Four Programming Languages Creating a Complete Website Scraper Application

Stephen Link

ISBN: 1511501510
ISBN-13: 978-1511501514

DEDICATION

I would like to give thanks to my God. Without Him, life would be unbearable. Thanks also to my wife who has supported me through the research and study time required to complete this book.

Many thanks go out to the teachers and mentors who have inspired the creative thought process and provided ideas for program material. Without others, this is a cold, cruel world.

CONTENTS

ACKNOWLEDGMENTS

I would like to give thanks to my God. Without Him, life would be unbearable. Thanks also to my wife who has supported me through the research and study time required to complete this book.

1 THE C# COMMAND LINE PROJECT

The code shown below is used for the command line version of the screen scraper program. The DOS-based EXE file can be automated with a batch file, Excel file or many other inventive methods that programmers may come up with. It could also be executed manually by typing each page into the command line prompt. We will start with showing you the first snippet of code.

```
// These are the required using statements which provide external functionality
using System;
using System.Collections.Generic;
using System.Linq;
using System.Text;
using System.Net;
using System.IO;
using System.Text.RegularExpressions;
```

The code can be typed into your C# command-line project (named web_scraper_console, in this example) if desired. Let's go through this code and explain the processing thoroughly. Starting at the top we have the "using" statements. As the code comment says, these are required to provide access to some of the external functions used in the program. Next, you will see the namespace, class and Main function. All of these will be created as the skeleton program when creating your project in Visual Studio.

```
namespace Web_Scraper_Console_
{
class Program
{
// Although the input arguments can be multiple, we are only processing one
static void Main(string[] args)
{
```

One thing that may require a little explanation is the "string[] args" which is a parameter in the Main function. Using this approach with a console program allows it to accept an array of parameters from the command line, such as "web_scraper_console index.php page1.aspx page2.html." This command will feed in an array of three pages to be processed, and you could modify the displayed code to utilize that functionality if desired. The program, as designed, only processes a single page; we will address a separate automation approach using Excel and VBA in a later chapter.

```
try
{
```

We use a try/catch block to catch any errors, and then move into "the meat" of the program.

```
string url = "http://www.linkemup.us/" + args[0] + ".aspx";
string strResult = "";
string progresult = "";
string outresult = "";
int charloc = 0;
int endloc = 0;
string delstr = "";
```

The first command in the program reads the only parameter allowed, args[0], and uses it to create the "url" string which will contain the full **U**niform **R**esource **L**ocator of the web page that will be processed. In this case, we are using my web site - www.linkemup.us, and automatically appending ".aspx" onto the page. A more functional approach is to allow the page extension to be entered in the command line, which will allow for the most flexibility. This code, as displayed, will not process completely because my web site is not based on ASP.Net pages. Also note that my web site is moving to a more descriptive domain name - www.ncwebdesignprogramming.com so the other site will probably not be available after October of 2014.

SIDE TRIP Let's examine the general functionality of your favorite web browser - Internet Explorer, Firefox, Chrome or one of the many others available. When you type a web site URL into the address line, it creates a webrequest which is sent to the target web server. A webresponse is also created to receive the response from the web server. Your browser then processes the response and displays the page that you had asked for.

The next few lines set up some processor "string" variables and a couple of location integers to be used in our program. The WebResponse and WebRequest provide the main functionality required by our program. What we are doing with these two objects is emulating the process of your web browser opening and displaying a page.

```
// This is preparing the application to read the web page into a webresponse object
WebResponse objResponse;
WebRequest objRequest = System.Net.HttpWebRequest.Create(url);
Console.WriteLine("Extracting...\nPlease Wait\n");
// We use GetResponse to read the webpage
objResponse = objRequest.GetResponse();
using (StreamReader sr = new StreamReader(objResponse.GetResponseStream()))
{
strResult = sr.ReadToEnd();
sr.Close();
}
```

After calling GetResponse on the objRequest, we now have the entire web page stored in our objResponse variable. Since objRequest is not truly in readable form, we have to use a combination of GetResponse() and GetResponseStream() to use a stream reader and assign the page contents to our strResult variable. We are doing a single call using the ReadToEnd function to read the entire page into our strResult variable. Because this is a single call, we close the streamreader within the same routine.

Why do we read the entire page into a single string variable? We take this approach so that we can extract the desired contents of that page in the most efficient manner. Imagine how complicated this program would be if we had to manage multiple variables or an array of strings.

Have you, as a student or programmer, experienced the power of the REGEX statement? This stands for "REGular EXpression" and it has the power to search, replace, and process a portion of any string. You may have heard this function called "wildcard on steroids." We will use the replace function of REGEX to do most of our processing work in this program. For the sake of detail, we will individually cover the aspects behind each of the statements below.

SIDE TRIP Try this experiment - on your next web browsing session, take a look at the raw source behind your favorite web page. It will probably have javascript, CSS, DIVs, comments and many other formatting and processing features. Although these mean something to the web browser, they mean nothing to the average user. These features also provide no functionality in the contents of a site migration scenario. Let's get back into the code …

```
// Remove scripts
strResult = Regex.Replace(strResult, "<script.*?</script>", "",
RegexOptions.Singleline | RegexOptions.IgnoreCase);
```

If you are an advanced student or seasoned programmer in any language, the functionality of the code shown above may be rather obvious. In case it is not, we will go into some detail now. First, let's note a difference between the REPLACE function and other, more familiar, append-style functions. Notice that each statement builds on the previous statement to parse out more of our raw page by replacing certain strings with nothing ("").

Now that we have a small explanation out of the way, we will look at the "Remove Scripts" statement. We examine the strResult variable for all occurrences of "<script...</script>" and remove them. Now, you may be wondering what the ".*?" is used for. The usage of ".*?" indicates that anything, or nothing, can occur between the beginning and ending script tags. The end result is the removal of all script code, whether it is JavaScript, VBScript or anything else contained within HTML <script></script> tags.

Two more options are used that require some explanation - Singleline and (|) IgnoreCase. IgnoreCase does exactly what it seems that it should - process all strings as lower case.

Singleline, on the other hand, requires a bit more explanation. Some strings may contain a "\n" in them. In most languages and applications, this will indicate to the program that a newline has been recognized, and that affects processing of the string. The Singleline option tells the program to consider the newline character part of the string, so it no longer has an effect on string processing.

```
// Remove inline stylesheets
strResult = Regex.Replace(strResult, "<style.*?</style>", "", RegexOptions.Singleline
| RegexOptions.IgnoreCase);
```

The code for removing inline stylesheets follows the same principle that you have already seen - regex replace. The only difference is the removal of anything within the HTML <style></style> tags.

SIDE TRIP What is a real life example of the cleanup that we have done so far? I am glad that you were pondering that thought. You can load any functional site on the web and view source. In that listing you will see lines such as

<script src="http://passets-cd.pinterest.com/webapp/js/app/desktop/bundle.c2facd24.js"></script>

And

<style>a:lang(ar),a:lang(kk-arab),a:lang(mzn),a:lang(ps),a:lang(ur){text-decoration:none}
/* cache key: enwiki:resourceloader:filter:minify-css:7:3904d24a08aa08f6a68dc338f9be277e */</style>

These are the lines removed so far due to the HTML tags that contain them. Now we will use the same approach to remove specific DIV elements. You will notice that we are removing any DIV names that begin with "level5," "level4" and "level3." We need to remove these specific DIVs because they exist in the body of the text that we are extracting.

```
// Remove three specific DIVs
strResult = Regex.Replace(strResult, "<div id='level5.*?</div>", "",
RegexOptions.Singleline | RegexOptions.IgnoreCase);
strResult = Regex.Replace(strResult, "<div id='level4.*?</div>", "",
RegexOptions.Singleline | RegexOptions.IgnoreCase);
strResult = Regex.Replace(strResult, "<div id='level3.*?</div>", "",
RegexOptions.Singleline | RegexOptions.IgnoreCase);
```

These lines are included as an example of the power of the web scraping program that we are building. If using the linkemup.us web page, these lines are not needed because the DIVs do not exist. Even though they do not exist, this causes no problem in execution of the code.

The ".*?" approach, shown previously, replaces the beginning and ending strings and everything between. In our next cleanup statements we will use some of the deeper functionality that regex can accomplish - pattern matching.

```
// Remove HTML tags
strResult = Regex.Replace(strResult, "</?[a-z][0-9]*[^<>]*>", "");
```

Let's take a look at the code to remove the HTML tags. The character "<" has to occur to begin the tag, while the "/" can occur 0 or 1 time. The "?" wildcard is the indicator of 0 or 1 occurrence of the character. Characters a to z and 0 to 9 can occur any number of times - this is the meaning of the "*" wildcard character which is placed after those specs. The next three characters inside of the brackets are explicit characters that can occur in the string, "^< >" but the "^" in front indicates that the bracket characters will not be replaced inside of the HTML tag. The closing character is the last in the HTML tag - ">"

What will this replace? It replaces all beginning HTML tags along with the matching end tags. Okay, why is additional processing required? It leaves the text between those tags. This also does not touch the non-standard tags such as comments and doctype, which are shown below.

```
// Remove HTML comments
strResult = Regex.Replace(strResult, "<!--(.|\\s)*?-->", "");
// Remove Doctype
strResult = Regex.Replace(strResult, "<!(.|\\s)?*>", "");
```

What and how will these two lines replace characters? The first line, as the comment states, will remove any HTML comments. In-line HTML comments begin with "<!--" so that is the beginning string searched for, and end with "-->" The included string "(.|\\s)" followed by the wildcard "*" means that any characters (other than a newline) and spaces can exist between the beginning and end string.

The Doctype tag begins with "<!" and it follows a similar process by replacing any doctype tags with an empty string.

```
strResult = strResult.Replace(" ", " ");
```

In the next line, we deviate from using the REGEX replace function and use a simple string replace function. Why does this work? It is because we are now replacing a single character string with no patterns or wildcards. In this case, we are searching for any non-breaking space characters and replacing them with a space.

So far, we have completed some rather impressive processing of our web page, but it still contains much more text than we want. In a normal desktop program, you could put a breakpoint here and examine the strResult string to see how much extra "stuff" that we have. Since this is a console program, you do not have that option, but you could achieve the same goal by using the "Console.WriteLine" command which is illustrated (and explained) as the last command in this program.

Since we do not want to use all of the processed text, what would be the best approach to get only the text that we want? You got it, start after a specific string and end before another string.

```
// the string below is the last menu item of the web site
// by starting after that string we are eliminating the header and menus
charloc = strResult.IndexOf("Create an account");
```

The first part of that approach is shown in this line of code, which uses the "IndexOf" function to find the first occurrence of the string that we will start after and assign that to the variable "charloc."

```
outresult = "---" + url + "---\r\n\r\n";
progresult = strResult.Substring(charloc + 17);
```

4

We now begin building the string which will be output from our web page processing. The first process is to create the first line with the URL being processed. This is the web address which was used in the very beginning of our program to read from. Next, we will use the "Substring" function to decide exactly where to begin reading the string. We add 17 to our "charloc" variable because that is the length of the string searched for and that variable is equal to the beginning location where it was found.

```
// the first string after the desired text is shown below. Stopping before this
// eliminates the footer text
endloc = progresult.IndexOf("Powered by");
progresult = progresult.Substring(1, endloc - 1);
```

Now we are again going to use "IndexOf" and "Substring" to determine where to stop in the string. Many functions will have multiple uses depending on how many variables are fed into them. "Substring" is one of those. Notice that in the first instance, we only used a single number, which indicated a begin position and included the entire string after that. Now we use two variables - a begin position of 1 and an end position of the string that we indicated. Also notice that we subtracted 1 from this location since CSharp is a zero-based language.

We have almost completed our processing of the page. If you were to write the current "progresult" string out to the console (using WriteLine), you may see many additional blank lines. If you are extracting this text for someone else to reformat and place into a new page, you want to eliminate as much of the extra work as possible, so we will remove any extra blanks that have been left from our processing.

```
// the section below removes additional blank lines that generally end up in
// the scraped text from a web page
StringReader delrdr = new StringReader(progresult);
while ((delstr = delrdr.ReadLine()) != null)
{
if (delstr.Trim() != "")
{
outresult = outresult + delstr + "\r\n";
}
}
```

First, we create a StringReader, which is used to process the individual lines in our "progresult" string. The "while" loop reads each line of the string until there are none left (!= null). We parse out the empty lines using the following "if" statement with a "Trim" to remove any spaces and compare it to an empty string. As long as the line is not empty, it is appended to our "outresult" variable.

Now that we have processed the desired text from our web page, we need to be able to present it in a format friendly enough for our end user. In this case, we use a ".txt" file extension, and the file will open in Notepad (for Windows, at least) by default. We could just as easily have used ".doc" so that it will open in Word.

Keep in mind that most end users are not tech savvy. They have become accustomed to clicking on a file and it opens. You accommodate this "tech laziness" by assigning an appropriate file extension. Any software written within the past decade should be perfectly comfortable with this approach.

```
// Write the file to the current directory with a .txt extension
System.IO.StreamWriter file = new StreamWriter(args[0] + ".txt");
file.WriteLine(outresult);
file.Close();
}
```

We create a StreamWriter with the variable of "file" which we will use for saving our processed page. Next, we build the filename using the argument that was fed in from the command line (args[0]) and the desired file extension. Using the "WriteLine" function will output the processed page to our file which was automatically opened with the previous line of code. We are sending the variable "outresult" to our file, which is the final string variable that we created earlier. In observance of standard coding practice, we now "Close" the file that we are writing to.

Hmmmmm ... so far we haven't really looked at error processing. We all know that students, and programmers, do not make mistakes - agreed? So I stretched the truth a tad. I am a programmer, after all.

```
catch (Exception ex)
{
Console.WriteLine(ex.Message,"Error");
}
}
}
}
```

The final section of our program contains the "catch" command. This is appropriate since the first processed line of code in our program was the corresponding "Try" command. As noted in the first paragraph, this is used for error processing. Although this particular approach only displays the word "Error" upon failure, you could test for specific error codes and display more meaningful instructions.

You have now created a console program which can save days of manual labor. Isn't it so nice to be involved in programming and be the hero of the company because of your hard work? You deserve a pat on the back and a big raise. If you are a student or beginning programmer, the pat on the back will give you some much needed recognition and the raise will help to pay down those student loans.

Hero? I have extracted the data from one page and have to run this again for each page. How is that a time saver? As the saying goes, "Very good, grasshopper," you have passed your first test. The time saving part comes from automating this process with an Excel VBA procedure or batch file. You don't know VBA? Don't worry, we will cover that in chapter 6.

2 THE C# DESKTOP PROJECT

It is assumed that you came to this chapter because you either favor the C# language for getting your job done most efficiently, or are interested in learning the language to make your job easier. Well, better coding and more flexibility are two of the reasons for selecting C# as my main programming language.

You may have created the C# console application, or it is possible that you skipped over to the desktop application section because "nobody does console apps anymore." If that quote happens to reflect your opinion, you are basically correct. Keep in mind, though, that console applications can be called and controlled from within other programs much easier. Our last chapter will display the approach of calling the console program from an Excel sheet using VBA code to process hundreds, maybe even thousands, of web pages with a few clicks of the mouse.

That is enough trying to impress you with the power and functionality available through console programs. Let's get into the C# desktop web scraper program. The screen shot below shows the layout of the tabs, text boxes, combo box, and buttons used in this program.

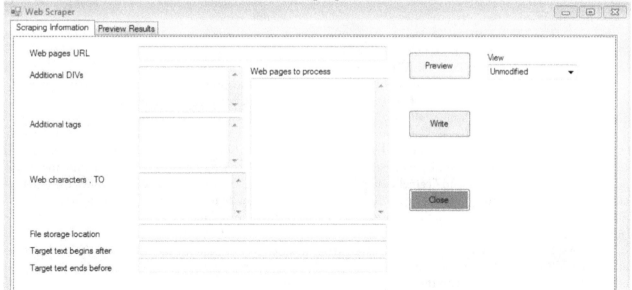

Our main container is a tab control with two tab pages. Most of the functionality is contained within the "Scraping Information" tab while the "Preview Results" tab contains a large multi-line scrolling textbox. We will start with the main functionality.

On this tab page you have nine labels, eight textboxes, three buttons and one combo box. You may be thinking that this does not look like eight textboxes. In that case, you are correct. Half of them don't look like the others - the reason is that they have vertical scrollbars and multiline turned on. You can see the contents of the nine labels, so let's cover the changes made to the other components in this screenshot.

The four normal text boxes, from the top down, are named txtURL, txtFile, txtBegin and txtEnd. Other than the size of these (330, 20), everything else is left at default. The three multiline textboxes on the left side are named txtDivs, txtTags, and txtChars while the larger multiline is named txtPages. You have already seen that these have multiline and vertical scrollbars turned on. There is nothing else special about these.

Just in case you are completely new to the Visual Studio and **I**ntegrated **D**evelopment **E**nvironment that it uses, let's cover the best way to get these controls onto your default form. Drag and drop, it is that simple. First, you drag a TabControl from the toolbox onto your screen and make it the size that you desire. In the Properties window for that tab control, you click on TabPages and the ellipsis button. Click the Add button twice to add two tab pages and then change the Text on those to "Scraping Information" and "Preview Results." Now that you have the TabControl on the screen and set up, you can select the "Scraping Information" tab and drag the controls shown in the above screenshot from the Toolbox.

I am sure that you have noticed the background color of the three buttons. That was achieved by changing only one property of each button - BackColor. The top button is named btnPreview and has been assigned the BackColor of "Yellow." It has a size of 84,38 and the Text is set to "Preview," as you can see on the screen. The middle button is the same size, has the name btnWrite and the BackColor of "GreenYellow." The bottom button is smaller (84,32) and has the BackColor of "OrangeRed." The name is btnClose.

The only remaining control that we have not covered is the combo box shown on the right side of the screenshot. It is named cboView and the Collection property contains two lines - "Unmodified" and "Processed Text." The Text property is set to "Unmodified" in order to display that as the default selection.

You may be wondering why the names of these controls are so important. To place them on the screen and make them look pretty the names don't matter at all. When we dive into the functionality behind each of these controls, you will experience the importance of properly naming your controls. As a matter of fact, without specific names you will have to deal with and identify label1, label9, label5 and so on. Since the label text is not modified in this program, they were left with the default names.

SIDE TRIP If you happen to be a programming student or job prospect, you may encounter the phrase "camel casing." That is my chosen method for identifying components in my program (cboView stands for combobox designating the VIEW selection). Using the camel casing approach, the first part of a variable name is lower cased while the following parts are capitalized (lblDateEntry is an excellent example). You may also learn of "pascal casing" in which you capitalize the first character of each part of the string. The previous example would be "LblDateEntry." The "upper case" approach is quite self-explanatory.

Why cover the casing subject? This is something that you may have paid attention to in class, or it may have just made sense to you, so you used a specific approach without knowing the name. As mentioned above, I use camel casing because it looks best and makes the most sense to my logical way of thinking. I was once in a job interview once and "camel casing" and "pascal casing" were mentioned. I had that deer-in-the-headlights look and the interviewer explained the difference. That made for an interesting lesson learned!

We have covered the casing methodologies, but why is casing important? It is not at all important in some languages, such as VB.Net in the next couple of chapters, while it is of extreme importance in C# and Java. In these two languages, "ToString" and "toString" are seen as two different variables because of the first letter difference. VB.Net, and others, are more forgiving in the casing aspect and will consider those two strings to be exactly the same. Enough with the explanations, on to the code …

Preview Button

Now we get into the really fun stuff - the code and functionality behind the visuals shown so far. Well, maybe not all of them are fun and exciting. Although the textboxes and combo box can have functionality tied to them, in this case they are just containers of information used in this program. The fun stuff is triggered by clicking one of the buttons. We will start with the btnPreview button and the two mouse events that are triggered - MouseDown and Click.

MouseDown is rather simple. It changes the text for the Preview button to "Please wait ..." That method is shown below.

```
private void btnPreview_MouseDown(object sender, MouseEventArgs e)
{
btnPreview.Text = "Please wait ...";
}
```

In case you are unfamiliar with adding code to an event using Visual Studio, we will cover that also. If you are in Form Design mode (as shown above), you select the button that will be modified. You should see a Properties area, which is usually anchored to the right under Solution Explorer. In the Properties section,

click on the Events icon   . Now if you double-click the empty section to the right of MouseDown, the method will automatically be named, created and assigned to the selected event. What this means is that you will see the code shown above without anything between the brackets (new, empty method). As long as the button has been named as suggested, start typing "btn" and the Visual Studio Intellicode will bring up a list of matches so that you can select btnPreview. Press the "." character and you will get another list which will have "Text" in it. As you have already seen, you can type the first couple of letters to narrow the selection list. Type the rest of the line, and don't forget to end it with a ";" character. That is a requirement of the C# language.

Well, that was an easy one. You have created your first method and made this program do something. You haven't done much yet, but at least you have more than a pretty picture. Don't worry, though. You have quite a bit of coding and knowledge to be gained before the program is finished.

First, some C# programming explanations may be useful to you. You have already seen the requirement that lines end with the semicolon (";") character. You have also seen the practice of enclosing procedures between brackets ({ ... }), and the fact that those brackets do not end with a semicolon. There are many other rules that you will need to follow, along with some "best practices" that will be pointed out. Here are just a few that are illustrated in the Click procedure below.

C# is a strongly-typed language. You will define variables prior to using them. You could define all of your variables at the top of the program, or you may prefer defining them just before being used.

Notice that we are using Strings, Ints and string arrays in this program, along with a few other types aimed at reading the web page and handling the text behind that page.

A basic principle of any programming language is the ability to loop, or iterate, through sets of data. If you have already completed chapter 1, a "while" loop has been introduced to you. We will add the "for" loop to your toolkit in this chapter.

Another very important aspect for programming logic is string manipulation. You will see a few differing approaches for building, parsing and modifying strings.

Placing comments in your code is always an excellent idea. You may know what it means now, as you are writing the code. You will likely forget what was done if changes are needed in six months or a year. Anyone who has to work on the program later will greatly appreciate those comments.

You may have some previous exposure to the use of variables. They are basically placeholders for some bit of data that your program will be manipulating. In this program, we start with the URL that was typed into the previously shown screen.

Let's move into some real functionality and take a look at the method called by the Click event, which is called btnPreview_Click.

```
private void btnPreview_Click(object sender, EventArgs e)
{
// This will display complete text or processed text in second tab
string baseurl = txtURL.Text;
```

Notice that our first line of code is a comment stating what will be done with the output of our method. In the next line we are declaring the baseurl variable as string and assigning to it the value of the string typed into the first textbox of our screen.

```
baseurl = baseurl.Replace("\\", "/");
if (!baseurl.EndsWith("/"))
{
baseurl = baseurl + "/";
}
if (!baseurl.ToLower().StartsWith("http"))
{
baseurl = "http://" + baseurl;
}
```

In these lines of code, we have used the "Replace" method to replace the "\" character with the other slash - "/". Did you notice that the first parameter in that statement has two backslash ("\") characters? That character is special and it is used for the purpose of "escaping" other characters. In other words, it can change the meaning of special characters that it is used in front of. If we wanted to add a newline to the string, we would use "\n" while a return can be appended to a string with the "\r" special character representation. These two are illustrated in a later section of code.

Why did we double the "\" character, though? By using two of these together, the .NET compiler knows that we actually mean to use the "\" character itself.

SIDE TRIP Compiler? Hmmmm, this is the first time I have heard of that. We won't get too technical with the definition, but the code that you see here, and type in yourself, is not executed by the program that you are running. That code is "compiled" into an executable program that you can run. The general process is to name the EXE file the same as your project. In the case of the project available for download (see appendix C), it will be called "WebScrDesktop.exe."

Now that we have that basic definition out of the way, let's dive into the rest of this section of code. You will notice the use of the EndsWith, StartsWith, and ToLower methods. These perform exactly what it seems like they should. With the EndsWith, we are checking for an ending "/" character on the string. If it does not exist (this is indicated by the "!" at the beginning of the string), we will add it with a simple "append" command. The logical next step is to convert the entire string to lower case using ToLower. This will ensure that we do not need to check for the existence of "http" or hTTp" or "HTTP."

I am sure that you get the picture. The string can be typed any way that the user desires, so we make accommodations for that. Once again, we are checking that it does NOT start with "http" and then add http:// to the front of the string using another simple append.

```
// change list of URLs into array
List<string> pgs = new List<string>();
pgs.AddRange(txtPages.Lines);
```

Notice that we have placed another comment to indicate the purpose of these couple of lines of code. We use another variable type called List<string>. As you have experienced so far, this means basically what it says - the variable "pgs" is a list of strings. In the next line of code we populate that list with each line that was entered into the txtPages textbox (remember, this has multi-line turned on). What have we done now? If we typed ten individual pages into the box, we now have the "pgs" list populated with ten items. We accomplished that population with a single AddRange command.

```
string[] pages = pgs.ToArray();
string strResult = "";
string progresult = "";
string outresult = "--" + baseurl + pages[0] + "--\r\n\r\n";
int charloc = 0;
```

```
int endloc = 0;
int y = 0;
string delstr = "";
```

You have already learned that variables need to be defined before they can be used. That is what we are doing with these eight lines of code. What you haven't been introduced to is an array. Notice that our first variable here is called "pages" and it is defined as a string[] (versus string, used elsewhere). This defines that variable as an array of strings. What is an array? Basically, it is a list, but the program does not see the list-type variable as an array. Because of this, we perform "ToArray" on the "pgs" variable to convert it into a string array.

In this section of code, you also get to experience the use of that array. Notice that we are appending "--, " baseurl, pages[0] and another string with some "escaped" characters. First, why do we use [0] behind the "pages" variable? Because it is an array and we are selecting the first item in that array. But this is zero, shouldn't the first be a "1"? Not in the C# language, it is a zero-based language. This means that arrays start with item [0] and locations within a string start with item 0. Yes, it requires a new mindset, but you can get the hang of it.

Now for a brief explanation of the previously promised "escape" sequence. At the end of this string, we are adding four of them - two pairs, actually. We have two sets of "\r\n" which basically tells our program that we want to end the line and start a new one. Since we are using two of these, we end the current line and add a blank line beneath it. So far, you have seen two of the escape sequences, and there are over a dozen more than you can research and find a use for.

```
for (int x = 0; x < pages.Count(); x++)
{
```

Now we are in "the meat" of the program, so it is time to slow the pace down a bit and give more detail in the functionality explanations. If you have gone through chapter one and built the functioning console application, you will probably recognize some of the code shown here - it is the same base logic with added functionality and capabilities afforded by a user interface.

The line above is known as a "FOR loop." The purpose is to begin with the first line in the "web pages to process" textbox and perform some processing with it. Once the end of the loop is reached, it will check to see if more lines exist and perform the process again and again until there are no more lines. Below that line of code you see an open brace ({). This indicates to our program that the loop processing starts now and goes until the matching close brace (}) is reached. Because of Ebook formatting rules, all text has to be left aligned, so it is not so easy to see where the end bracket happens to be. In your Visual Studio editor, the sections will be indented and easily identifiable.

```
WebResponse objResponse;
WebRequest objRequest = System.Net.HttpWebRequest.Create(baseurl+pages[x]);
objResponse = objRequest.GetResponse();
```

These three lines work together to load the current web page, as it was entered into the "web pages to process" textbox. First, we create a WebResponse object (named objResponse) which is used to store the response received from the web page as it is loaded. The second variable, objRequest, is a WebRequest which is combined with an HttpWebRequest to retrieve the web page from its host. We determine the **U**niform **R**esource **L**ocator by combining the entry into the "web pages URL" (baseurl) with the current line that we are processing, indicated by "x." Finally, we get to use the GetResponse() method of objRequest to read the page contents into objResponse. Now that we have the web page in memory, it is time to do something with it.

```
using (StreamReader sr = new StreamReader(objResponse.GetResponseStream()))
{
strResult = sr.ReadToEnd();
```

This is another statement that may be familiar to you from chapter 1. The purpose of a "using" statement is to automatically implement "try … catch" error handling and give us a more reliable method of handling an object. In this case, the object that we are handling is a StreamReader named "sr."

Did you just catch a deviation from the requirement that a variable is defined **before** it is used? That was a good, but not completely accurate, catch. We are actually declaring the "sr" variable, athough it is declared within the line of code that it is used.

So what does this StreamReader do? I am glad that you were pondering that. It uses a GetResponseStream method to process the contents of the web page (currently in "objResponse") into the previously defined strResult string.

```
// Close and clean up the StreamReader
sr.Close();
}
```

Now we close the "sr" object. Since it was opened for reading (or writing, appending, etc), it has to be closed. We also close the "using" section of code with a closing brace (}). Notice that this acts as the closing brace for the closest open. Even though we are closing out the "using" section of code, we are still within the "for" loop.

```
if (cboView.SelectedItem.ToString() == "Processed Text")
{
```

We have just opened an "if" statement. This has the same function as your logical decision making that is performed every day - if I have a couple of donuts for breakfast, (then) I need to walk an extra mile during lunch. You could also add to that - "(else) I can walk my dog an extra mile tonight." That covers the simplicity of an if-then-else statement although you can string these together and create some monster-sized logic. If you see a need for more than a few of these used together, the "select … case" statement will probably be a much better option. You can research that command on your own and decide where it fits.

Anyway, back to our "if" statement. This is looking at the selection made with the "dropdown" which is labeled "View." Since you have only two options in this box, we check to see if "Processed text" was selected. If it was, then we process a section of code. If the other option - "Unmodified" was selected, a separate section of code is executed. Once again, the code between { and } is executed in either instance.

```
// Remove scripts
strResult = Regex.Replace(strResult, "<script.*?</script>", "",
RegexOptions.Singleline | RegexOptions.IgnoreCase);
// Remove inline stylesheets
strResult = Regex.Replace(strResult, "<style.*?</style>", "", RegexOptions.Singleline
| RegexOptions.IgnoreCase);
```

If you are an advanced student or seasoned programmer in any language, the functionality of the code shown above may be rather obvious. In case it is not, we will go into some detail. First, let's note a difference between the REPLACE function and other, more familiar, append-style functions. Notice that each statement builds on the previous statement to parse out more of our raw page by replacing certain strings with nothing ("").

Now that we have a small explanation out of the way, we will look at the "Remove Scripts" statement. We examine the strResult variable for all occurrences of "<script...</script>" and remove them. Now, you may be wondering what the ".*?" is used for. The usage of ".*?" indicates that anything, or nothing, can occur between the beginning and ending script tags. The end result is the removal of all script, whether it is JavaScript, VBScript or anything else contained within HTML <script></script> tags.

Two more options are used that require some explanation - Singleline and (|) IgnoreCase. IgnoreCase does exactly what it seems that it should - process all strings as lower case. Singleline, on the other hand, requires a bit more explanation. Some strings may contain a "\n" in them. In most languages and applications, this will indicate to the program that a newline has been recognized. That affects processing of the string. The Singleline option tells the program to consider the newline character part of the string, so it no longer has an effect on string processing.

The code for removing inline stylesheets follows the same principle that you have already seen - regex replace. The only difference is the removal of anything within the HTML <style></style> tags.

SIDE TRIP What is a real life example of the cleanup that we have done so far? I am glad that you were pondering that thought. You can load any functional site on the web and view source. In that listing you will see lines such as

```
<script src="http://passets-cd.pinterest.com/webapp/js/app/desktop/bundle.c2facd24.js"></script>
```

And

```
<style>a:lang(ar),a:lang(kk-arab),a:lang(mzn),a:lang(ps),a:lang(ur){text-decoration:none}
/* cache key: enwiki:resourceloader:filter:minify-css:7:3904d24a08aa08f6a68dc338f9be277e */</style>
```

These are the lines removed so far due to the HTML tags that are contained in them. You may recognize these explanations if you have already completed chapter one. Yes, the lines and explanations are exactly the same.

```
// remove DIVs here, if any
if (txtDivs.Text.Trim() != "")
{
```

Here we see another "if" statement. This time we are checking to see if anything was entered into the "txtDivs" textbox. This is accomplished by looking at the Text in the box and performing a Trim on it. The purpose of Trim is to remove all leading and trailing spaces. If anything is entered into the textbox, it will not return an empty string (!=) and processing will continue with the next line. Otherwise, the program skips all lines until the corresponding closing brace.

```
List<string> dvs = new List<string>();
dvs.AddRange(txtDivs.Lines);
string[] divs = dvs.ToArray();
```

We are using the same approach that was used to create the array of web pages from our "txtPages" textbox. Create the list, populate it, and convert it to an array.

```
for (y = 0; y < divs.Count(); y++)
{
strResult = Regex.Replace(strResult, "<div id='" + divs[y] + ".*?</div>", "",
RegexOptions.Singleline | RegexOptions.IgnoreCase);
}
}
```

You should now be familiar with the "for" loop and the Replace method. Notice that we are replacing a specific DIV which was entered into the "txtDivs" textbox. This gives us the opportunity to remove as many DIVs as necessary. As long as we use a begin and end text string, the only DIVs that will need to be removed will be between those two strings. Also notice the two closing braces in this code. It is closing the "for" loop and the "if" statement. The next line of code is where the processing continues in case the "if" statement is actually false (empty txtDivs textbox).

```
// remove other tags, if any
if (txtTags.Text.Trim() != "")
{
List<string> tgs = new List<string>();
```

```
tgs.AddRange(txtTags.Lines);
string[] tags = tgs.ToArray();
for (y = 0; y < tags.Count(); y++)
{
strResult = Regex.Replace(strResult, tags[y] + ".*?</div>", "",
RegexOptions.Singleline | RegexOptions.IgnoreCase);
}
}
```

This uses the exact same logic as the DIVs, except that it is used for specific HTML tags. The pages that you are extracting the text from may contain non-breaking spaces. In that case, you would enter " " into the txtTags textbox. Others that you may want to use are "<" (<), "&" (&) or more special HTML characters. Whether they are needed will depend on whether they are used within the desired web page.

```
// Remove HTML tags
strResult = Regex.Replace(strResult, "</?[a-z][a-z0-9]*[^<>]*>", "");
// Remove HTML comments
strResult = Regex.Replace(strResult, "<!--(.|\\s)*?-->", "");
// Remove Doctype
strResult = Regex.Replace(strResult, "<!(.|\\s)*?>", "");
```

Now we get to remove the standard HTML tags (between the brackets) using some of the deeper functionality that regex can accomplish - pattern matching. The character "<" has to occur to begin the tag, while the "/" can occur 0 or 1 time. The "?" wildcard is the indicator of 0 or 1 occurrence of the character. Characters a to z and 0 to 9 can occur any number of times - this is the meaning of the "*" wildcard character which occurs after these specs. The next three characters inside of the brackets are explicit characters that can occur in the string, "< >" but the "^" in front indicates that the bracket characters will not be replaced inside of the HTML tag. The closing character is the last in the HTML tag - ">"

What will this replace? It replaces all beginning HTML tags along with the matching end tags. Okay then, why is additional processing required? It leaves the text between those tags. This also does not touch the non-standard tags such as comments and doctype. The next line, as the comment states, will remove any HTML comments. In-line HTML comments begin with "<!--" so that is the beginning string searched for, and end with "-->" The included string "(.|\\s)" followed by the wildcard "*" means that any characters (other than a newline) and spaces can exist between the beginning and end string. The Doctype tag begins with "<!" and it follows a similar process by replacing any doctype tags with an empty string.

```
// if web character replacement, it goes here
if (txtChars.Text.Trim() != "")
{
string fromtext = "";
string totext = "";
for(y=0;y<txtChars.Lines.Count();y++)
{
fromtext = txtChars.Lines[y].Substring(0, txtChars.Lines[y].IndexOf(","));
totext = txtChars.Lines[y].Substring(txtChars.Lines[y].IndexOf(",") + 1);
strResult = strResult.Replace(fromtext,totext);
}
}
}
```

Using the "webscraper" program, you have the ability to replace any strings with anything else that you may desire. Maybe the scraped pages have a number of employees set to 100 and you want to automatically change that to 110. If so, you would enter 100,110 in a single line of the txtChars textbox.

That is the purpose of this section of code, but how is it accomplished? Good pondering. First, we have to break the "from" and "to" text out of the comma-delimited line. In both cases, we look for the comma with "IndexOf" and use Substring to parse out the two variables. Now that we have the from/to text, it is a simple Replace on the strResult variable. Notice that we are closing the "for," "if" and the "if" that checked to see if "Processed Text" had been selected. If not, processing falls through to the following "else" procedure.

```
else
{
outresult = strResult;
}
```

Just like the processing in the preceding "if" statement, we could have many lines of processing within the "else" procedure. In this case, we only need one line which sets the "outresult" variable to be displayed in the Preview tab. The general idea is if "Unmodified" is selected, you also do not enter begin or end text.

You may be wondering, "What purpose does 'Unprocessed' have?" Good question. As an end result, the unprocessed text is quite useless. In the beginning of the process, however, you can view this code to pick out the begin/end text, DIVs to remove, additional tags and character changes needed within the program.

```
if (txtBegin.Text.Trim() != "")
{
charloc = strResult.IndexOf(txtBegin.Text.Trim());
progresult = strResult.Substring(charloc + txtBegin.Text.Trim().Length-1);
```

So far in this routine, we have determined that something was entered into the txtBegin textbox. We search for that string within strResult using IndexOf and store that into the "charloc" variable. Now that we know the location of that beginning string, we use Substring to start at the desired location within "strResult" and assign the new string to "progresult." The proper starting point is actually the found location of the "txtBegin" string plus the length of that string minus 1. Since we are only using one parameter of Substring, the result begins at that point and returns the remainder of the string.

Remember, C# is a zero-based language. This makes it necessary to subtract 1 from lengths and a few other properties.

```
if (txtEnd.Text.Trim() != "")
{
endloc = progresult.IndexOf(txtEnd.Text.Trim());
progresult = progresult.Substring(1, endloc - 1);
}
```

Now we check to see if an ending string was entered. If so, we check for the existence of it within progresult using IndexOf. Once again, we use Substring, this time with a start and end parameter. We start at the second character (zero-based) and use the rest of the "progresult" string until it encounters the end string (minus 1). If we had left this variable empty in our use of the program, it will still execute fine. By leaving out a specific end string, we will keep many extra pieces of information since well-designed web sites will use a footer section for contact, address and other information.

If you were to look at the "progresult" string now, you will probably notice many undesired blank lines that were generated by all of the replace commands. This is not truly desirable, so we have a routine that will read progresult one line at a time and assign the line to the "outresult" variable only if it is not empty.

```
StringReader delrdr = new StringReader(progresult);
while ((delstr = delrdr.ReadLine()) != null)
{
if (delstr.Trim() != "")
{
outresult = outresult + delstr + "\r\n";
}
```

```
}
}
```

As stated, this routine will read each line of the "progresult" variable by assigning it to a StringReader named "delrdr." Within the "while" statement, we are using ReadLine to individually read each line until we have no more. The line is being read into the "delstr" string variable. Inside of the while process, we are using Trim to determine that the line is not empty (see previous explanation of Trim, if necessary). If not empty, the line is appended to the "outresult" string variable with the carriage return-line feed escape sequences. Notice the three closing braces.

```
if (x < pages.Count()-1)
{
outresult = outresult + "\r\n\r\n--" + pages[x + 1] + "--\r\n\r\n";
}
}
```

Now we have finished processing the current page. The "x" variable is the current line that we are on and it is being compared to the total pages count (minus 1). Let's say that there was only one web page entered, that would be index 0 and x is currently 0. Pages.count is 1but when we subtract 1 from that, the "if" statement is false and we fall through to the display of our results, shown below.

If two web pages were entered, and this is the first time through the routine, x is still equal to 0. The count of pages is now 2 and zero is less than 1 so we append the name of the next web page and proceed back through the routine again.

```
txtPreview.Text = outresult;
tabControl1.SelectTab(1);
btnPreview.Text = "Preview";
}
```

What are we doing to finish up the processing of the Preview function? We have the processed web page text in the "outresult" variable, so we assign that to txtPreview.Text so that we can preview the output. We have a problem, though. You know from the first paragraph in this chapter that "the 'Preview Results' tab contains a large multi-line scrolling textbox," but you have not been told the name of it - that would be "txtPreview." In order to display that tab, we perform a SelectTab and use index 1 (second tab). We also set the Text for btnPreview back to "Preview" (remember, we had set it to "Please wait …").

SIDE TRIP Let's recap what we have done. As previously mentioned, you can view the source of any web site, and it will look similar to the code shown below. Yes, this is a portion of the LinkEmUp EBooks page.

<span class="showHere">You are here: </span><a href="/" class="pathway">Home</a> <img src="/templates/beez5/images/system/arrow.png" alt="" /> <span>LinkEmUp Published EBooks</span></div>

</div>

<div class="left1 leftbigger" id="nav"><div class="moduletable_menu">

<h3><span class="backh"><span class="backh2"><span class="backh3">This Site</span></span></span></h3><ul class="menu">

<li class="item-435"><a href="/" >Home</a></li><li class="item-233"><a href="/login" >Login</a></li><li class="item-448"><a href="/administrator" target="_blank" >Site Administrator</a></li><li class="item-469"><a href="/projects" >Projects</a></li><li class="item-483"><a href="http://astore.amazon.com/puliemup-20" >My Amazon Store</a></li><li class="item-472"><a href="/bail-management" >Bail Bond</a></li><li class="item-480"><a href="/mobile-app-development" >Mobile App Development</a> … <a href="/press-release-menu" >Press Release Listing</a></li><li class="item-482 current active"><a href="/linkemup-published-ebooks" >LinkEmUp

Published EBooks</a></li><li class="item-484"><a href="http://blog.linkemup.us" >LinkEmUp
Blog</a></li></ul>
    </div></div><!-- end navi -->
    <div id="wrapper2" ><div id="main">
    <div id="system-message-container">
    </div><div class="item-page">
    <h2><a href="/linkemup-published-ebooks">   EBooks (Publishing div)</a></h2>
    <ul class="actions"><li class="print-icon">
    <a href="/linkemup-published-ebooks?tmpl=component&print=1&page=" title="Print"
onclick="window.open(this.href,'win2','status=no,toolbar=no,scrollbars=yes,titlebar=no,menubar=no,resiza
ble=yes,width=640,height=480,directories=no,location=no'); return false;" rel="nofollow"><img
src="/media/system/images/printButton.png" alt="Print" /></a></li>
    <li class="email-icon"><a
href="/component/mailto/?tmpl=component&template=beez5&link=7cff5138f0c6c6908df825c6
e73d73e0e003ba96" title="Email"
onclick="window.open(this.href,'win2','width=400,height=350,menubar=yes,resizable=yes'); return
false;"><img src="/media/system/images/emailButton.png" alt="Email" /></a></li></ul>
    <dl class="article-info"><dt class="article-info-term">Details</dt>
    <dd class="category-name">Category: <a href="/linkemup-published-ebooks/78-
projects">Projects</a> </dd>
    <dd class="published"> Published on Wednesday, 29 January 2014 20:38 </dd>
    <dd class="createdby"> Written by Administrator</dd>
    <dd class="hits">Hits: 547</dd></dl><p> LinkEmUp Publishes EBooks</p>
    <p>We have created Bible study material aimed at high school age and young adults. This material will be
spread across ten volumes and will cover five or six lessons per EBook. The EBooks are available in Kindle,
Nook, and other formats. See below for the list and links where these can be purchased.</p>
    ... Next ></a></li>
    </ul></div></div><!-- end main --></div><!-- end wrapper -->
    <div class="wrap"></div></div> <!-- end contentarea --></div><!-- back -->
    </div><!-- all --><div id="footer-outer"><div id="footer-sub">
    <div id="footer">
    <p>Powered by <a href="http://www.joomla.org/">Joomla!®</a></p>
    </div><!-- end footer -->

After we run the program on it

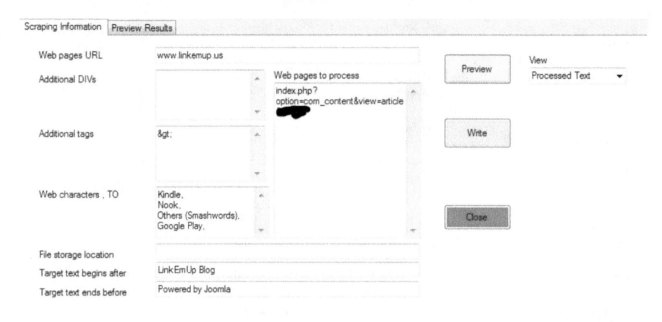

we see ...

--http://www.linkemup.us/index.php?option=com_content&view=article&id=103--

EBooks (Publishing div)

Details

Category: Projects

Published on Wednesday, 29 January 2014 20:38

Written by Administrator

Hits: 556

LinkEmUp Publishes EBooks

We have created Bible study material aimed at high school age and young adults. This material will be spread across ten volumes and will cover five or six lessons per EBook. The EBooks are available in , , and other formats. See below for the list and links where these can be purchased.

Control Your Windows 7 View: Use a Single Wallpaper Across All of Your Screens

Complete, Responsive, Mobile App Design Using Visual Studio: Integrating MySQL Database into your web page (Free 2/21,22,23 through KDP Select)

HTML5, CSS3, Javascript and JQuery Mobile Programming: Beginning to End Cross-Platform App Design

Making the Most of Your Money in a Recovering EconomyFree at Smashwords and

Vol 1 - You Are the Potter's Clay: Mold Your Spirit with a study in Proverbs

Vol 2 - You Are the Potter's Clay: Mold Your Spirit with a study in Matthew

Vol 3 - You Are the Potter's Clay: Mold Your Spirit with a study in John

Vol 4 - You Are the Potter's Clay: Mold Your Spirit with another study in John

Vol 5 - You Are the Potter's Clay: Mold Your Spirit with a study in Hebrews

Shop Amazon - Top Rated in Store++ Shop Amazon - Movers & Shakers in Store ++ Shop Amazon - Hot New Releases in Store ++ Shop Amazon - Best Sellers in Store ++ Sign up for Amazon prime benefits

Next

Notice the use of the additional tag and the web characters. Since the HTML for the links was removed, it left the link text for the different book sites. We remove the link text with the four lines of "web characters." There was also a ">" left at the end of the "Next" word, so we removed that using the "Additional tags" option. More "web character" entries could have been used to remove the "monetization" Amazon text, the word "Next," and a couple more changes, but I am sure that you get the idea of how useful this can be.

That was a lot of work, and we have only been through the Preview button. Don't worry, though, the Write button uses the same logic plus a little extra code to write the results to a file.

Write Button

When looking at the code behind btnWrite, we will be leaving out much of the detail due to the exact code structure and logic when compared to the Preview function. You will be presented with all of the code, should you desire to type it in. It is suggested that, if you are using the code entry opportunity to better understand it, you should copy the code previously typed into the Preview button and modify as necessary. Let's begin with the MouseDown event ...

```
private void btnWrite_MouseDown(object sender, MouseEventArgs e)
{
btnWrite.Text = "Please wait ...";
}
```

Now we get into the code behind the Click event ...

```
private void btnWrite_Click(object sender, EventArgs e)
{
// This will write complete text files and display processed text in second tab
string baseurl = txtURL.Text;
if (txtFile.Text.Trim() != "")
{
baseurl = baseurl.Replace("\\", "/");
if (!baseurl.EndsWith("/"))
{
baseurl = baseurl + "/";
}
if (!baseurl.ToLower().StartsWith("http"))
{
baseurl = "http://" + baseurl;
}
// change list of URLs into array
List<string> pgs = new List<string>();
pgs.AddRange(txtPages.Lines);
string[] pages = pgs.ToArray();
string strResult = "";
string progresult = "";
string outresult = "--" + baseurl + pages[0] + "--\r\n\r\n";
string outfile = "--" + pages[0] + "--\r\n\r\n";
int charloc = 0;
int endloc = 0;
int y = 0;
string delstr = "";
for (int x = 0; x < pages.Count(); x++)
{
WebResponse objResponse;
WebRequest objRequest = System.Net.HttpWebRequest.Create(baseurl + pages[x]);
objResponse = objRequest.GetResponse();
using (StreamReader sr = new StreamReader(objResponse.GetResponseStream()))
{
strResult = sr.ReadToEnd();
```

```
// Close and clean up the StreamReader
sr.Close();
}
if (cboView.SelectedItem == "Processed Text")
{
// Remove scripts
strResult = Regex.Replace(strResult, "<script.*?</script>", "",
RegexOptions.Singleline | RegexOptions.IgnoreCase);
// Remove inline stylesheets
strResult = Regex.Replace(strResult, "<style.*?</style>", "", RegexOptions.Singleline
| RegexOptions.IgnoreCase);
// remove DIVs here, if any
if (txtDivs.Text.Trim() != "")
{
List<string> dvs = new List<string>();
dvs.AddRange(txtDivs.Lines);
string[] divs = dvs.ToArray();
for (y = 0; y < divs.Count(); y++)
{
strResult = Regex.Replace(strResult, "<div id='" + divs[y] + ".*?</div>", "",
RegexOptions.Singleline | RegexOptions.IgnoreCase);
}
}
// remove other tags, if any
if (txtTags.Text.Trim() != "")
{
List<string> tgs = new List<string>();
tgs.AddRange(txtTags.Lines);
string[] tags = tgs.ToArray();
for (y = 0; y < tags.Count(); y++)
{
strResult = Regex.Replace(strResult, tags[y] + ".*?</div>", "",
RegexOptions.Singleline | RegexOptions.IgnoreCase);
}
}
// Remove HTML tags
strResult = Regex.Replace(strResult, "</?[a-z][a-z0-9]*[^<>]*>", "");
// Remove HTML comments
strResult = Regex.Replace(strResult, "<!--(.|\\s)*?-->", "");
// Remove Doctype
strResult = Regex.Replace(strResult, "<!(.|\\s)*?>", "");
// if web character replacement, it goes here
if (txtChars.Text.Trim() != "")
{
string fromtext = "";
string totext = "";
for (y = 0; y < txtChars.Lines.Count(); y++)
{
fromtext = txtChars.Lines[y].Substring(0, txtChars.Lines[y].IndexOf(","));
totext = txtChars.Lines[y].Substring(txtChars.Lines[y].IndexOf(",") + 1);
strResult = strResult.Replace(fromtext, totext);
}
}
}
```

```
if (txtBegin.Text.Trim() != "")
{
charloc = strResult.IndexOf(txtBegin.Text.Trim());
// read each line at top and delete as long as it is blank
progresult = strResult.Substring(charloc + 17);
if (txtEnd.Text.Trim() != "")
{
endloc = progresult.IndexOf(txtEnd.Text.Trim());
progresult = progresult.Substring(1, endloc - 1);
}
StringReader delrdr = new StringReader(progresult);
while ((delstr = delrdr.ReadLine()) != null)
{
if (delstr.Trim() != "")
{
```

Until this point, nothing has changed in the processing of the web page that has been read in. This is exactly the same as the Preview code. It is at this point that we begin to see code added to enable the creation of a text file (using the variable outfile) containing the same output that we see in the Preview screen.

```
outresult = outresult + delstr + "\r\n";
outfile = outfile + delstr + "\r\n";
}
}
string outdir = txtFile.Text.Trim();
if(!outdir.EndsWith("\\"))
{
outdir = outdir + "\\";
}
```

We are using a technique, which should be rather familiar to you by now, to check for a "\" character at the end of the directory entered ("outdir") to be used for writing the file(s). The statement was made that we will write out what we see in the Preview screen. That is almost, but not 100%, accurate. We will write what we see into individual files. If you process three pages, you will see all three in the Preview screen, but will have three files written out with the web page name.

Another difference between this code and Preview is that we are not handling the "Unmodified" selection. This is based on the belief that you do not want to write the entire web page to a file. Of course, if that were a possibility, the previous approach could be implemented and would work well.

```
System.IO.StreamWriter file = new StreamWriter(outdir + pages[x].Replace(".","_") +
".txt");
file.WriteLine(outfile);
file.Close();
```

We have used a StreamWriter to create the file and use Replace to replace any "." characters with "_" in the file name. Using the WriteLine method of file, we write out the file. Then the file is closed, and we have finished writing the file.

```
if (x < pages.Count() - 1)
{
outresult = outresult + "\r\n\r\n--" + pages[x + 1] + "--\r\n\r\n";
outfile = "--" + pages[x + 1] + "--\r\n\r\n";
}
}
}
```

Just like the Preview approach, we are continuing with another entry in the Preview text. For the file to be written to disk, we are starting new instead of appending to the existing string. You will notice a difference between these two lines of code.

```
txtPreview.Text = outresult;
tabControl1.SelectTab(1);
btnWrite.Text = "Write";
}
else
{
MessageBox.Show("You have to enter a write location for the file");
}
}
```

Other than the presence of btnWrite (versus btnPreview) and a message being displayed if Write was clicked with no location for file creation, this code is exactly the same as we saw in Preview. We have introduced a bit of new functionality with the MessageBox.Show command. As is the case with so many of the Visual Studio commands, it does exactly what it seems should be done - display the message contained in the quotes.

SIDE TRIP Since you saw the difference between the raw web site and processed text in the previous section, we will show an example of the additional functionality added to btnWrite. To produce the files shown below, we entered three web pages into the program and used "C:\Outweb" in the txtFile textbox. If desired, the code could be added to check for the existence of the directory entered and create it if necessary. In this instance, we are expecting the directory to exist.

Name	Date modified	Type	Size
associnscience_aspx.txt	6/14/2014 12:29 PM	Text Document	4 KB
businessadministration_aspx.txt	6/14/2014 12:29 PM	Text Document	3 KB
cosmetology_aspx.txt	6/14/2014 12:29 PM	Text Document	2 KB

3 THE VB.NET COMMAND LINE PROJECT

' These are the required import statements which provide external functionality
Imports System.Net
Imports System.IO
Imports System.Text
Imports System.Text.RegularExpressions

The code can be typed into your VB.Net command-line project (named WebScraperVBCon) if desired. Let's go through this and explain the processing thoroughly. Starting at the top we have the "Imports" statements. As the code comment says, these are required to provide access to some of the external functions used in the program. Next, you will see the Module and Sub functions. All of these will be created as the skeleton program when creating your project in Visual Studio.

Module Module1
Sub Main()

If you followed through chapter one, you will notice a couple of differences right away - the use of a different comment character (' versus \\) and the absence of semicolons (;) to end the lines. Another difference that may require a little explanation is the use of "GetCommandLineArgs." which is a parameter in the Main Subroutine. Using this approach with a console program allows it to accept an array of parameters from the command line, such as "WebScraperVBCon index.php page1.aspx page2.html." This command will feed in an array of three pages to be processed, and you could modify this code to utilize that functionality if desired. The program, as designed, only processes a single page; we will address a separate automation approach using Excel and VBA in a later chapter.

Try
Dim inpargs() As String = Environment.GetCommandLineArgs()
Dim url As String = "http://www.linkemup.us/" + inpargs(1) + ".aspx"

We use a try/catch block to catch any errors, and then move into "the meat" of the program. The first two commands in the program read the only input parameter processed, the "inpargs" variable, and uses it to create the "url" string which will contain the full **U**niform **R**esource **L**ocator of the web page that will be processed. In this case, we are using my web site - www.linkemup.us, and automatically appending ".aspx" onto the page. A more functional approach is to allow the page extension to be entered in the command line, which will allow for the most functionality. This code, as displayed, will not process completely because my web site is not based on ASP.Net pages. Also note that my web site is moving to a more descriptive domain name - www.ncwebdesignprogramming.com so the other site will probably not be available after October of 2014.

You may also realize that this uses the index location of "1" for the input arguments. VB.Net considers the program name itself as location zero.

SIDE TRIP Let's examine the general functionality of your favorite web browser - Internet Explorer, Firefox, Chrome or one of the many others available. When you type a web site URL into the address line, it creates a webrequest which is sent to the target web server. A webresponse is also created to receive the response from the web server. Your browser then processes the response and displays the page that you had asked for.

```
Dim strResult As String = ""
Dim progresult As String = ""
Dim outresult As String = ""
Dim charloc As Integer = 0
Dim endloc As Integer = 0
Dim delstr As String = ""
```

The next few lines set up some processor "string" variables and a couple of location integers to be used in our program.

```
Dim objResponse As WebResponse
Dim objRequest As WebRequest = HttpWebRequest.Create(url)
Console.WriteLine("Extracting...\nPlease Wait\n")
Console.WriteLine(url)
objResponse = objRequest.GetResponse()
Using sr As StreamReader = New StreamReader(objResponse.GetResponseStream())
strResult = sr.ReadToEnd()
' Close and clean up the StreamReader
sr.Close()
End Using
```

The WebResponse and WebRequest provide the main functionality required by our program. What we are doing with these two objects is emulating the process of your web browser opening and displaying a page.

After calling GetResponse on the objRequest, we now have the entire web page stored in our objResponse variable. The next couple of lines use the "WriteLine" command to display messages on the screen for us. First, we enclose a "wait" message in quotes, and then we display the web address (url) that we will be using. Since objRequest is not truly in readable form, we have to use a combination of GetResponse() and GetResponseStream() to use a stream reader and assign the page contents to our strResult variable. We are doing a single call using the ReadToEnd function to read the entire page into our strResult variable. Because this is a single call, we close the streamreader within the same routine.

Another difference between Visual Basic and the previous C# language is the use of an "End" statement to indicate the end of a routine instead of the open and close braces ({ .. })

Why do we read the entire page into a single string variable? We take this approach so that we can extract the desired contents of that page in the most efficient manner. Imagine how troublesome this process would be if we had to manage multiple variables or an array of strings.

Have you, as a student or programmer, experienced the power of the REGEX statement? This stands for "REGular EXpression" and it has the power to search, replace, and process a portion of any string. You may have heard this function called "wildcard on steroids." We will use the replace function of REGEX to do most of our processing work in this program. For the sake of detail, we will individually cover the aspects behind each of the statements below.

SIDE TRIP Try this experiment. On your next web browsing session, take a look at the raw source behind your favorite web page. It will probably have javascript, CSS, DIVs, comments and many other formatting and processing features. Although these mean something to the web browser, they mean nothing to the average user. These features also provide no functionality in the contents of a site migration scenario. Let's get back into the code …

```
' Remove scripts
strResult = Regex.Replace(strResult, "<script.*?</script>", "", RegexOptions.Singleline And
RegexOptions.IgnoreCase)
```

If you are an advanced student or seasoned programmer in any language, the functionality of the code shown above may be rather obvious. In case it is not, we will go into some detail now. First, let's note a difference between the REPLACE function and other, more familiar, append-style functions. Notice that each statement builds on the previous statement to parse out more of our raw page by replacing certain strings with nothing ("").

Now that we have a small explanation out of the way, we will look at the "Remove Scripts" statement. We examine the strResult variable for all occurrences of "<script...</script>" and remove them. Now, you may be wondering what the ".*?" is used for. The usage of ".*?" indicates that anything, or nothing, can occur between the beginning and ending script tags. The end result is the removal of all script code, whether it is JavaScript, VBScript or anything else contained within HTML <script></script> tags.

Two more options are used that require some explanation - Singleline and IgnoreCase. IgnoreCase does exactly what it seems that it should - process all strings as lower case. Singleline, on the other hand, requires a bit more explanation. Some strings may contain a "\n" in them. In most languages and applications, this will indicate to the program that a newline has been recognized, and that affects processing of the string. The Singleline option tells the program to consider the newline character part of the string, so it no longer has an effect on string processing.

You may have noticed another difference between the VB and C# code - the use of "And" versus "|". This is one of the many syntax differences between the two languages. Fortunately, since all Visual Studio languages are based on the .Net programming framework, a majority of the code will easily transport between languages.

```
' Remove inline stylesheets
strResult = Regex.Replace(strResult, "<style.*?</style>", "", RegexOptions.Singleline And
RegexOptions.IgnoreCase)
```

The code for removing inline stylesheets follows the same principle that you have already seen - regex replace. The only difference is the removal of anything within the HTML <style></style> tags.

SIDE TRIP What is a real life example of the cleanup that we have done so far? I am glad that you were pondering that thought. You can load any functional site on the web and view source. In that listing you will see lines such as

```
<script src="http://passets-cd.pinterest.com/webapp/js/app/desktop/bundle.c2facd24.js"></script>
```

And

```
<style>a:lang(ar),a:lang(kk-arab),a:lang(mzn),a:lang(ps),a:lang(ur){text-decoration:none}
/* cache key: enwiki:resourceloader:filter:minify-css:7:3904d24a08aa08f6a68dc338f9be277e */</style>
```

These are the lines removed so far due to the HTML tags that contain them. Now we will use the same approach to remove specific DIV elements. You will notice that we are removing any DIV names that begin with "level5," "level4" and "level3." We need to remove these specific DIVs because they exist in the body of the text that we are extracting.

```
// Remove three specific DIVs
```

```
    strResult = Regex.Replace(strResult, "<div id='level5.*?</div>", "", RegexOptions.Singleline And
RegexOptions.IgnoreCase)
    strResult = Regex.Replace(strResult, "<div id='level4.*?</div>", "", RegexOptions.Singleline And
RegexOptions.IgnoreCase)
    strResult = Regex.Replace(strResult, "<div id='level3.*?</div>", "", RegexOptions.Singleline And
RegexOptions.IgnoreCase)
```

These lines are included as an example of the power of the web scraping program that we are building. If using the linkemup.us web page, these lines are not needed because the DIVs do not exist. Even though they do not exist, this causes no problem in execution of the code.

The ".*?" approach, shown previously, replaces the beginning and ending strings and everything between. In our next cleanup statements we will use some of the deeper functionality that regex can accomplish - pattern matching.

```
    ' Remove HTML tags
    strResult = Regex.Replace(strResult, "</?[a-z][a-z0-9]*[^<>]*>", "")
```

Let's take a look at the code to remove the HTML tags. The character "<" has to occur to begin the tag, while the "/" can occur 0 or 1 time. The "?" wildcard is the indicator of 0 or 1 occurrence of the character. Characters a to z and 0 to 9 can occur any number of times - this is the meaning of the "*" wildcard character. The next three characters inside of the brackets are explicit characters that can occur in the string, "^< >" but the "^" in front indicates that the bracket characters will not be replaced inside of the HTML tag. The closing character is the last in the HTML tag - ">"

What will this replace? It replaces all beginning HTML tags along with the matching end tags. Okay then, why is additional processing required? It leaves the text between those tags. This also does not touch the non-standard tags such as comments and doctype, which are shown below.

```
    ' Remove HTML comments
    strResult = Regex.Replace(strResult, "<!--(.|\\s)*?-->", "")
    ' Remove Doctype
    strResult = Regex.Replace(strResult, "<!(.|\\s)*?>", "")
```

What and how will these next two lines replace characters? The first line, as the comment states, will remove any HTML comments. In-line HTML comments begin with "<!--" so that is the beginning string searched for, and end with "-->" The included string "(.|\\s)" followed by the wildcard "*" means that any characters (other than a newline) and spaces can exist between the beginning and end string.

The Doctype tag begins with "<!" and it follows a similar process by replacing any doctype tags with an empty string.

```
    ' Remove excessive whitespace
    strResult = strResult.Replace(" ", " ")
    strResult = strResult.Replace("&quot;", "'")
```

In the next couple of lines, we deviate from using the REGEX replace function and use a simple string replace function. Why does this work? It is because we are now replacing a single character string with no patterns or wildcards. In this case, we are searching for any non-breaking space characters and replacing them with a space. For extra functionality, we replace the quote character with " ' "

So far, we have completed some rather impressive processing of our web page, but it still contains much more text than we want. In a normal desktop program, you could put a breakpoint here and examine the strResult string to see how much extra "stuff" that we have. Since this is a console program, you do not have that option, but you could achieve the same goal by using the "Console.WriteLine" command which is illustrated, and explained, as the last command in this program.

Since we do not want to use all of the processed text, what would be the best approach to get only the text that we want? You got it, start after a specific string and end before another string.

```
' the string below is the last menu item of the web site
' by starting after that string we are eliminating the header and menus
charloc = strResult.IndexOf("Create an account")
```

The first part of that approach is shown in our next line of code, which uses the "IndexOf" function to find the first occurrence of the string that we will start after and assign that to the variable "charloc."

```
outresult = "---" + url + "---" + vbCrLf + vbCrLf
progresult = strResult.Substring(charloc + 17)
```

We now begin building the string which will be output from our web page processing. The first thing to do is create the first line with the URL being processed. This is the web address which was used in the very beginning of our program to read from. Next, we will use the "Substring" function to decide exactly where to begin reading the string. We add 17 to our "charloc" variable because that is the length of the string searched for and that variable is equal to the beginning location where it was found.

Did you work with the C# code in chapter 1? If so, you should recognize a difference in the next line of code - vbCrLf instead of the "\r\n" escape string. This accomplishes the same result of adding a line break.

```
' the first string after the desired text is shown below. Stopping before this
' eliminates the footer text
endloc = progresult.IndexOf("Powered by")
progresult = progresult.Substring(1, endloc - 1)
```

Now we are again going to use "IndexOf" and "Substring" to determine where to stop in the string. Many functions will have multiple uses depending on how many variables are fed into them. "Substring" is one of those. Notice that in the first instance, we only used a single number, which indicated a begin position and included the entire string after that. Now we use two variables - a begin position of 1 and an end position of the string that we indicated.

We have almost completed our processing of the page. If you were to write the current "progresult" string out to the console (using WriteLine), you may see many additional blank lines. If you are extracting this text for someone else to reformat and place into a new page, you want to eliminate as much of the extra work as possible, so we will remove any extra blanks that have been left from our processing.

```
' the section below removes additional blank lines that generally end up in
' the scraped text from a web page
Dim delrdr As StringReader = New StringReader(progresult)
While True
delstr = delrdr.ReadLine()
If (delstr Is Nothing) Then
Exit While
End If
If (delstr.Trim() <> "") Then
outresult = outresult + delstr + vbCrLf
End If
End While
```

First, we create a StringReader, which is used to process the individual lines in our "progresult" string. The "while" loop reads each line of the string until there are none left (Is Nothing). We parse out the empty lines using the following "if" statement with a "Trim" to remove any spaces and compare it to an empty string. As long as the line is not empty, it is appended to our "outresult" variable.

```
' Write the file to the current directory with a .txt extension
Dim file As StreamWriter = New StreamWriter(inpargs(1) + ".txt")
file.WriteLine(outresult)
file.Close()
```

Now that we have processed the desired text from our web page, we need to be able to present it in a format friendly enough for our end user. In this case, we use a ".txt" file extension, and the file will open in Notepad (for Windows, at least) by default. We could just as easily have used ".doc" so that it will open in Word.

Keep in mind that most end users are not tech savvy. They have become accustomed to clicking on a file and it opens. You accommodate this "tech laziness" by assigning an appropriate file extension. Any software written within the past decade should be perfectly comfortable with this approach.

We create a StreamWriter with the variable of "file" which we will use for saving our processed page. We build the filename using the argument that was fed in from the command line (inpargs(1)) and the desired file extension. Using the "WriteLine" function will output the processed page to our file which was automatically opened with the previous line of code. We are sending the variable "outresult" to our file, which is the final string variable above, which was created earlier. In observance of standard coding practice, we now "Close" the file that we are writing to.

Hmmmmm … so far we haven't really looked at error processing. We all know that students, and programmers, do not make mistakes - agreed? So I stretched the truth a tad. I am a programmer, after all.

```
Catch ex As Exception
Console.WriteLine(ex.Message, "Error")
End Try
End Sub
End Module
```

The final section of our program contains the "catch" command. This is appropriate since the first processed line of code in our program was the corresponding "Try" command. As noted in the first paragraph, this is used for error processing. Although this particular approach only displays the word "Error" upon failure, you could test for specific error codes and display more meaningful instructions.

You have now created a console program which can save days of manual labor. Isn't it so nice to be involved in programming and be the hero of the company because of your hard work? You deserve a pat on the back and a big raise. If you are a student or beginning programmer, the pat on the back will give you some much needed recognition and the raise will help to pay down those student loans.

Hero? I have extracted the data from one page and have to run this again for each page. How is that a time saver? As the saying goes, "Very good, grasshopper," you have passed your first test. The time saving part comes from automating this process with an Excel VBA procedure or batch file. You don't know VBA? Don't worry, we will cover that in chapter 6.

4 THE VB.NET DESKTOP PROJECT

It is assumed that you came to this chapter because you either favor the VB language for getting your job done most efficiently, or are interested in learning the language to make your job easier.

You may have created the VB console application, or it is possible that you skipped over to the desktop application section because "nobody does console apps anymore." If that quote happens to reflect your opinion, you are basically correct. Keep in mind, though, that console applications can be called and controlled from within other programs much easier. Our last chapter will display the approach of calling the console program from an Excel sheet using VBA code to process hundreds, maybe even thousands, of web pages with a few clicks of the mouse.

That is enough of trying to impress you with the functionality and power available through console programs. Let's get into the VB desktop web scraper program. The screen shot below shows the layout of the tabs, text boxes, combo box, and buttons used in this program.

Our main container is a tab control with two tab pages. Most of the functionality is contained within the "Scraping Information" tab while the "Preview Results" tab contains a large multi-line scrolling textbox. We will start with the main functionality.

On this tab page you have nine labels, eight textboxes, three buttons and one combo box. You may be thinking that this does not look like eight textboxes. In that case, you are correct. Half of them don't look like the others - the reason is that they have vertical scrollbars and multiline turned on. You can see the contents of the nine labels, so let's cover the changes made to the other components in this screenshot.

The four normal text boxes, from the top down, are named txtURL, txtFile, txtBegin and txtEnd. Other than the size of these (330, 20), everything else is left at default. The three multiline textboxes on the left side are named txtDivs, txtTags, and txtChars while the larger multiline is named txtPages. You have already seen that these have multiline and vertical scrollbars turned on. There is nothing else special about these.

Just in case you are completely new to the Visual Studio and **I**ntegrated **D**evelopment **E**nvironment that it uses, let's cover the best way to get these controls onto your default form. Drag and drop, it is that simple. First, you drag a TabControl from the toolbox onto your screen and make it the size that you desire. In the Properties window for that tab control, you click on TabPages and the ellipsis button. Click the Add button twice to add two tab pages and then change the Text on those to "Scraping Information" and "Preview Results." Now that you have the TabControl on the screen and set up, you can select the "Scraping Information" tab and drag the controls shown in the above screenshot from the Toolbox.

I am sure that you have noticed the background color of the three buttons. That was achieved by changing only one property of each button - BackColor. The top button is named btnPreview and has been assigned the BackColor of "Yellow." It has a size of 84,38 and the Text is set to "Preview," as you can see on the screen. The middle button is the same size, has the name btnWrite and the BackColor of "GreenYellow." The bottom button is smaller (84,32) and has the BackColor of "OrangeRed." The name is btnClose.

The only remaining control that we have not covered is the combo box shown on the right side of the screenshot. It is named cboView and the Collection property contains two lines "Unmodified" and "Processed Text." The Text property is set to "Unmodified" in order to display that as the default selection.

You may be wondering why the names of these controls is so important. To place them on the screen and make them look pretty the names don't matter at all. If you want to easily identify the control in the coding process, proper name assignment is extremely important. When we dive into the functionality behind each of these controls, you will experience how important it is to properly name your controls. As a matter of fact, without specific names you will have to deal with and identify label1, label9, label5 and so on. Since the label text is not modified in this program, they were left with the default names.

SIDE TRIP If you happen to be a programming student or job prospect, you may encounter the phrase "camel casing." That is my chosen method for identifying components in my program (cboView stands for combobox designating the VIEW selection). Using the camel casing approach, the first part of a variable name is lower cased while the following parts are capitalized (lblDateEntry is an excellent example). You may also learn of "pascal casing" in which you capitalize the first character of each part of the string. The previous example would be "LblDateEntry." The "upper case" approach is quite self-explanatory.

Why cover the casing subject? This is something that you may have paid attention to in class, or it may have just made sense to you, so you used a specific approach without knowing the name. As mentioned above, I use camel casing because it looks best and makes the most sense to my logical way of thinking. I was once in a job interview once and "camel casing" and "pascal casing" were mentioned. I had that deer-in-the-headlights look and the interviewer explained the difference. That made for an interesting lesson learned!

We have covered the casing methodologies, but why is casing important? It is not at all important in some languages, as is the case with VB.Net, while it is of extreme importance in C# and Java. In these two languages, "ToString" and "toString" are seen as two different variables because of the first letter difference. For code portability, you should get in the habit of observing proper casing regardless of the language used. Enough with the explanations, on to the code …

Preview Button

Now we get into the really fun stuff - the code and functionality behind the visuals shown so far. Well, maybe not all of them are fun and exciting. Although the textboxes and combo box can have functionality tied to them, they are just containers of information as they are used in this program. The fun stuff is triggered by clicking one of the buttons. We will start with the btnPreview button and the two mouse events that are triggered - MouseDown and Click.

MouseDown is rather simple. It changes the text for the Preview button to "Please wait ..." That method is shown below.

```
Private Sub btnPreview_MouseDown(sender As System.Object, e As
System.Windows.Forms.MouseEventArgs) Handles btnPreview.MouseDown
    btnPreview.Text = "Please wait ..."
End Sub
```

Here we see another differentiation from the C# coding approach - Handles. This command allows assignment of a single section of code to multiple elements. For instance, you could assign this sub to be triggered by btnPreview and btnWrite. If taking this approach, you could check the "sender" and use that to assign the text of the correct button.

In case you are unfamiliar with adding code to an event, we will cover that also. If you are in Form Design mode (as shown above), you select the button that will be modified. You should see a Properties area, which is usually anchored to the right under Solution Explorer. In the Properties section, click on the Events icon

. Now if you double-click the empty section to the right of MouseDown, the method will automatically be named, created and assigned to the selected event. What this means is that you will see the code shown above without anything before the "End Sub" command (new, empty method). If you have followed the same naming convention, start typing "btn" and the Visual Studio Intellicode will bring up a list of matches so that you can select btnPreview. Press the "." character and you will get another list which will have "Text" in it. Just like you have already seen, you can type the first couple of letters to narrow the selection list. Type the rest of the line, and be sure that it does not end with a ";" character. The VB language does not require or recognize that as the end of line.

Well, that was an easy one. You have created your first method and made this program do something. You haven't done much yet, but at least you have more than a pretty picture. Don't worry, though. You have quite a bit of coding and learning to be done before the program is finished.

First, some VB programming explanations may be useful to you. You have seen the practice of closing procedures with the END ... statement. There are many other rules that you will need to follow, along with some "best practices" that will be pointed out. Here are just a few that are illustrated in the Click procedure below.

VB uses a hybrid approach to typing. You will define variables prior to using them. You could define all of your variables at the top of the program, or you could use the approach of defining them just before being used. You can use a VAR type which will assume the variable type from the initial assignment.

Notice that we are using Strings, Ints and string arrays in this program, along with a few other types aimed at reading the web page and handling the text behind that page.

A basic principle of any programming language is the ability to loop, or iterate, through sets of data. If you have already completed previous chapters, you have seen various looping structures.

Another very important aspect for programming logic is string manipulation. You will see a few differing approaches for building, parsing and modifying strings.

Placing comments in your code is always an excellent idea. You may know what it means now, as you are writing the code. You will likely forget what, and why, a specific approach was taken if changes are needed in six months or a year. Anyone who has to work on the program later will greatly appreciate those comments.

You may have some exposure to the use of variables. They are basically placeholders for some bit of data that your program will be manipulating. In this program, we start with the URL that was typed into the previously introduced screen.

Let's move into some real functionality and take a look at the method called by the Click event, which is called btnPreview_Click.

Private Sub btnPreview_Click(sender As System.Object, e As System.EventArgs) Handles btnPreview.Click

```
' This will display complete text or processed text in second tab
Dim baseurl As String = txtURL.Text
```

Notice that our first line of code is a comment stating what will be done with the output of our method. In the next line we are declaring the baseurl variable as string and assigning to it the value of the string typed into the first textbox of our screen.

```
baseurl = baseurl.Replace("\\", "/")
If (Not baseurl.EndsWith("/")) Then
baseurl = baseurl + "/"
End If
If (Not baseurl.ToLower().StartsWith("http")) Then
baseurl = "http://" + baseurl
End If
```

In these lines of code, we have used the "Replace" method to replace the "\" character with the other slash - "/". Did you notice that the first parameter in that statement has two backslash ("\") characters? That character is special and it is used for the purpose of "escaping" other characters. In other words, it can change the meaning of any character it is used in front of.

Why did we double the "\" character, though? By using two of these together, the .NET compiler knows that we actually mean to use the "\" character itself.

Compiler? Hmmmm, this is the first that I have heard of that. We won't get too technical with the definition, but the code that you see here, and type in yourself, is not executed by the IDE program that you are running. That code is "compiled" into an executable program that you can run. The general process is to name the EXE file the same as your project. In the case of the project available for download (see appendix C), it will be called "WebScraperVB.exe."

Now that we have another basic definition out of the way, let's dive into the rest of this section of code. You will notice the use of the EndsWith, StartsWith, and ToLower methods. These perform exactly what it seems like they should. With the EndsWith, we are checking for an ending "/" character on the string. If it does not exist (this is indicated by the "!" at the beginning of the string), we will add it with a simple "append" command. The logical next step is to convert the entire string to lower case using ToLower. This will ensure that we do not need to check for the existence of "http" or hTTp" or "HTTP."

I am sure that you get the picture. The string can be typed any way that the user desires, so we make accommodations for that flexibility. Once again, we are checking that it does NOT start with "http" and then add http:// to the front of the string using another simple append.

```
' change list of URLs into array
Dim pgs As List(Of String) = New List(Of String)
pgs.AddRange(txtPages.Lines)
```

Notice that we have placed another comment to indicate the purpose of these couple of lines of code. We use another variable type called List(Of string). As you have experienced so far, this means basically what it says - the variable "pgs" is a list of strings. In the next line of code we populate that list with each line that was entered into the txtPages textbox (remember, this has multi-line turned on).

What have we done now? If we typed ten individual web pages into the box, we now have the "pgs" list populated with ten items. We accomplished that population with a single AddRange command.

So far you haven't been introduced to an array. Notice our initialization and use of the variable called "pgs" and it is defined as a List(Of String) (versus string, used elsewhere). This defines that variable as an array of strings. What is an array? Basically, it is a list. Because of this, it is well suited to accept the "array" of individual lines within the txtPages textbox.

```
Dim strResult As String = ""
Dim progresult As String = ""
Dim outresult As String = "--" + baseurl + pgs(0).ToString() + "--" + vbCrLf + vbCrLf
Dim charloc As Integer = 0
Dim endloc As Integer = 0
Dim y As Integer = 0
Dim delstr As String = ""
```

You have already learned that variables need to be defined before they can be used. That is what we are doing with these seven lines of code. In this section of code, you also get to experience the use of that array. Notice that we are appending "--, " baseurl, pages(0) and another string with some "escaped" characters. First, why do we use (0) behind the "pages" variable? Because it is an array and we are selecting the first item in that array. But this is zero, shouldn't the first be a "1"? Not in the VB language, it is zero-based. This means that arrays start with item (0) and locations within a string start with item 0. Yes, it requires a new mindset, but you can get the hang of it.

To end the current line, we use vbCrLf. Since we are using two of these, we end the current line and add a blank line beneath it.

```
For x As Integer = 0 To pgs.Count() - 1
```

Now we are in "the meat" of the program, so it is time to slow the pace down a bit and give more detail in the functionality explanations. If you have gone through previous chapters and built the functioning applications, you will probably recognize some of the code shown here - it is the same base logic with added functionality and capabilities afforded by a user interface.

The line above is known as a "FOR loop." The purpose is to begin with the first line in the "web pages to process" textbox and perform some processing with it. Once the end of the loop is reached, it will check to see if more lines exist and perform the process again and again until there are no more lines. Processing starts now and goes until the matching END statement is reached. Because of Ebook formatting rules, all text has to be left aligned, so it is not so easy to see where the end statement happens to be. In your Visual Studio editor, the sections will be indented and easily identifiable.

```
Dim objResponse As WebResponse
Dim objRequest As WebRequest = System.Net.HttpWebRequest.Create(baseurl + pgs(x).ToString())
objResponse = objRequest.GetResponse()
```

These three lines work together to load the current web page, as it was entered into the "web pages to process" textbox. First, we create a WebResponse object (named objResponse) which is used to store the response received from the web page as it is loaded. The second variable, objRequest, is a WebRequest which is combined with an HttpWebRequest to retrieve the web page from its host. We determine the Uniform Resource Locator by combining the entry into the "web pages URL" (baseurl) with the current line that we are processing, indicated by "x." Finally, we get to use the GetResponse() method of objRequest to read the page contents into objResponse. Now that we have the web page in memory, it is time to do something with it.

```
Using sr As StreamReader = New StreamReader(objResponse.GetResponseStream())
strResult = sr.ReadToEnd()
```

This is another statement that may be familiar to you from previous chapters. The purpose of a "using" statement is to automatically implement "try ... catch" error handling and give us a more reliable method of handling an object. In this case, the object that we are handling is a StreamReader named "sr."

Did you just catch a deviation from the requirement that a variable is defined **before** it is used? That was a good, but not completely accurate, catch. We are actually declaring the "sr" variable, athough it is declared within the line of code that it is used.

So what does this StreamReader do? I am glad that you were pondering that. It uses a GetResponseStream method to process the contents of the web page (currently in "objResponse") into the previously defined strResult string.

```
' Close and clean up the StreamReader
sr.Close()
End Using
```

Now we close the "sr" object. Since it was opened for reading (or writing, appending, etc), it has to be closed. We also close the "using" section of code with an End Using statement. Even though we are closing out the "using" section of code, we are still within the "for" loop.

```
If cboView.SelectedItem = "Processed Text" Then
```

We have just opened an "if" statement. This has the same function as your logical decision making that is performed every day - if I have a couple of donuts for breakfast, (then) I need to walk an extra mile during lunch. You could also add to that - "(else) I can walk my dog an extra mile tonight." That covers the simplicity of an if-then-else statement although you can string these together and create some monster-sized logic. If you see a need for more than a few of these strung together, the "select ... case" statement will probably be a much better option. You can research that command on your own and decide where it fits well.

Anyway, back to our "if" statement. This is looking at the selection made with the "dropdown" which is labeled "View." Since you have only two options in this box, we check to see if "Processed text" was selected. If it was, then we process a section of code. If the other option - "Unmodified" was selected, a separate section of code is executed. Once again, the code between If and End If (or Else) is executed.

```
' Remove scripts
strResult = Regex.Replace(strResult, "<script.*?</script>", "", RegexOptions.Singleline And
RegexOptions.IgnoreCase)
' Remove inline stylesheets
strResult = Regex.Replace(strResult, "<style.*?</style>", "", RegexOptions.Singleline And
RegexOptions.IgnoreCase)
```

If you are an advanced student or seasoned programmer in any language, the functionality of the code shown above may be rather obvious. In case it is not, we will go into some detail. First, let's note a difference between the REPLACE function and other, more familiar, append-style functions. Notice that each statement builds on the previous statement to parse out more of our raw page by replacing certain strings with nothing ("").

Now that we have a small explanation out of the way, we will look at the "Remove Scripts" statement. We examine the strResult variable for all occurrences of "<script...</script>" and remove them. Now, you may be wondering what the ".*?" is used for. The usage of ".*?" indicates that anything, or nothing, can occur between the beginning and ending script tags. The end result is the removal of all script, whether it is JavaScript, VBScript or anything else contained within HTML <script></script> tags.

Two more options are used that require some explanation - Singleline And IgnoreCase. IgnoreCase does exactly what it seems that it should - process all strings as lower case. Singleline, on the other hand, requires a bit more explanation. Some strings may contain a "\n" in them. In most languages and applications, this will indicate to the program that a newline has been recognized. That affects processing of the string. The Singleline option tells the program to consider the newline character part of the string, so it no longer has an effect on string processing.

The code for removing inline stylesheets follows the same principle that you have already seen - regex replace. The only difference is the removal of anything within the HTML <style></style> tags.

SIDE TRIP What is a real life example of the cleanup that we have done so far? I am glad that you were pondering that thought. You can load any functional site on the web and view source. In that listing you will see lines such as

```
<script src="http://passets-cd.pinterest.com/webapp/js/app/desktop/bundle.c2facd24.js"></script>
```

And

```
<style>a:lang(ar),a:lang(kk-arab),a:lang(mzn),a:lang(ps),a:lang(ur){text-decoration:none}
/* cache key: enwiki:resourceloader:filter:minify-css:7:3904d24a08aa08f6a68dc338f9be277e */</style>
```

These are the lines removed so far due to the HTML tags that are contained in them. You may recognize these explanations if you have already completed previous chapters. Yes, the lines and explanations are exactly the same.

```
' remove DIVs here, if any
If txtDivs.Text.Trim() <> "" Then
```

Here we see another "if" statement. This time we are checking to see if anything was entered into the "txtDivs" textbox. This is accomplished by looking at the Text in the box and performing a Trim on it. The purpose of Trim is to remove all leading and trailing spaces. If anything is entered into the textbox, it will not return an empty string (<>) and processing will continue with the next line. Otherwise, the program skips all lines until the corresponding End If statement.

```
Dim dvs As List(Of String) = New List(Of String)
dvs.AddRange(txtDivs.Lines)
```

We are using the same approach that was used to create the array of web pages from our "txtPages" textbox. Create the list, populate it, and convert it to an array.

```
For y = 0 To dvs.Count() - 1
strResult = Regex.Replace(strResult, "<div id="" & dvs(y).ToString() & ".*?</div>", "",
RegexOptions.Singleline And RegexOptions.IgnoreCase)
Next y
End If
```

You should be familiar with the "for" loop and the Replace method. Notice that we are replacing a specific DIV which was entered into the "txtDivs" textbox. This gives us the opportunity to remove as many DIVs as necessary. As long as we use a begin and end text string, the only DIVs that will need to be removed will be between those two strings. Also notice the Next and End If statements in this code. It is closing the "for" loop and the "if" statement. The next line of code is where the processing continues in case the "if" statement is actually false (empty txtDivs textbox).

```
' remove other tags, if any
If txtTags.Text.Trim() <> "" Then
Dim tgs As List(Of String) = New List(Of String)
tgs.AddRange(txtTags.Lines)
For y = 0 To tgs.Count() - 1
strResult = Regex.Replace(strResult, tgs(y).ToString() + ".*?</div>", "", RegexOptions.Singleline And
RegexOptions.IgnoreCase)
Next
End If
```

This uses the exact same logic as the DIVs, except that it is used for specific HTML tags. The pages that you are extracting the text from may contain non-breaking spaces. In that case, you would enter " " into the txtTags textbox. Others that you may want to use are "<" (<), "&" (&) and more. Whether they are needed will depend on whether they are used within the desired web page.

```
' Remove HTML tags
strResult = Regex.Replace(strResult, "</?[a-z][0-9]*[^<>]*>", "")
' Remove HTML comments
strResult = Regex.Replace(strResult, "<!--(.|\\s)*?-->", "")
' Remove Doctype
strResult = Regex.Replace(strResult, "<!(.|\\s)*?>", "")
```

Now we get to remove the standard HTML tags (between the brackets) using some of the deeper functionality that regex can accomplish - pattern matching. The character "<" has to occur to begin the tag, while the "/" can occur 0 or 1 time. The "?" wildcard is the indicator of 0 or 1 occurrence of the character. Characters a to z and 0 to 9 can occur any number of times - this is the meaning of the "*" wildcard character which appears after those two specs. The next three characters inside of the brackets are explicit characters that can occur in the string, "^< >" but the "^" in front indicates that the bracket characters will not be replaced inside of the HTML tag. The closing character is the last in the HTML tag - ">"

What will this replace? It replaces all beginning HTML tags along with the matching end tags. Okay then, why is additional processing required? It leaves the text between those tags. This also does not touch the non-standard tags such as comments and doctype. The next line, as the comment states, will remove any HTML comments. In-line HTML comments begin with "<!--" so that is the beginning string searched for, and end with "-->" The included string "(.|\\s)" followed by the wildcard "*" means that any characters (other than a newline) and spaces can exist between the beginning and end string. The Doctype tag begins with "<!" and it follows a similar process by replacing any doctype tags with an empty string.

```
' if web character replacement, it goes here
If txtChars.Text.Trim() <> "" Then
Dim fromtext As String = ""
Dim totext As String = ""
For y = 0 To txtChars.Lines.Count() - 1
fromtext = txtChars.Lines(y).Substring(0, txtChars.Lines(y).IndexOf(","))
totext = txtChars.Lines(y).Substring(txtChars.Lines(y).IndexOf(",") + 1)
strResult = strResult.Replace(fromtext, totext)
Next y
End If
End If
```

Using the "webscraper" program, you have the ability to replace any strings with anything else that you may desire. Maybe the scraped pages have a number of employees set to 100 and you want to automatically change that to 110. If so, you would enter 100,110 in a single line of the txtChars textbox.

That is the purpose of this feature, but how is it accomplished? Good pondering. First, we have to break the "from" and "to" text out of the comma-delimited line. In both cases, we look for the comma with "IndexOf" and use Substring to parse out the two variables. Now that we have the from/to text, it is a simple Replace on the strResult variable. Notice that we are closing the "for," "if" and the "if" that checked to see if "Processed Text" had been selected. If not, processing falls through to the following "else" procedure.

```
Else
outresult = strResult
End If
```

Just like the processing in the preceding "if" statement, we could have many lines of processing within the "else" procedure. In this case, we only need one line which sets the "outresult" variable to be displayed in the Preview tab. The general idea is if "Unmodified" is selected, you also do not enter begin or end text.

You may be wondering, "What purpose does 'Unprocessed' have?" Good question. As an end result, the unprocessed text is quite useless. In the beginning of the process, however, you can view this code to pick out the begin/end text, DIVs to remove, additional tags and character changes needed within the program.

```
If txtBegin.Text.Trim() <> "" Then
charloc = strResult.IndexOf(txtBegin.Text.Trim())
progresult = strResult.Substring(charloc + 17)
```

So far in this routine, we have determined that something was entered into the txtBegin textbox. We search for that string within strResult using IndexOf and store that into the "charloc" variable. Now that we know the location of that beginning string, we use Substring to start at the desired location within "strResult" and assign the new string to "progresult." The proper starting point is actually the found location of the "txtBegin" string plus the length of that string minus 1. Since we are only using one parameter of Substring, the result begins at that point and returns the remainder of the string.

Remember, VB is a zero-based language. This makes it necessary to subtract 1 from lengths and a few other properties.

```
If txtEnd.Text.Trim() <> "" Then
endloc = progresult.IndexOf(txtEnd.Text.Trim())
progresult = progresult.Substring(1, endloc - 1)
End If
```

Now we check to see if an ending string was entered. If so, we check for the existence of it within progresult using IndexOf. Once again, we use Substring, this time with a start and end parameter. We start at the second character (zero-based) and use the rest of the "progresult" string until it encounters the end string (minus 1). If we had left this variable empty in our use of the program, it will still execute fine. By leaving out a specific end string, we will keep many extra pieces of information since well-designed web sites will use a footer section for contact, address and other information.

If you were to look at the "progresult" string now, you will probably notice many undesired blank lines that were generated by all of the replace with an empty string. This is not truly desirable, so we have a routine that will read progresult one line at a time and assign the line to the "outresult" variable only if it is not empty.

```
Dim delrdr As StringReader = New StringReader(progresult)
' read each line at top and delete as long as it is blank
While True
delstr = delrdr.ReadLine()
If delstr Is Nothing Then
Exit While
End If
If delstr.Trim() <> "" Then
outresult = outresult + delstr + vbCrLf
End If
End While
End If
```

As stated, this routine will read each line of the "progresult" variable by assigning it to a StringReader named "delrdr." Within the "while" statement, we are using ReadLine to individually read each line until we have no more. The line is being read into the "delstr" string variable. Inside of the while process, we are using Trim to determine that the line is not empty (see previous explanation of Trim, if necessary). If not empty, the line is appended to the "outresult" string variable with the carriage return-line feed escape sequences. Notice the three closing statements.

```
If x < pgs.Count() - 1 Then
outresult = outresult + vbCrLf + vbCrLf + "--" + pgs(x + 1).ToString() + "--" + vbCrLf + vbCrLf
End If
Next x
```

Now we have finished processing the current page. The "x" variable is the current line that we are on and it is being compared to the total pages count (minus 1). Let's say that there was only one web page entered, that would be index 0 and x is currently 0. Pages.count is 1but when we subtract 1 from that, the "if" statement is false and we fall through to the display of our results, shown below.

If two web pages were entered, and this is the first time through the routine, x is still equal to 0. The count of pages is now 2 and zero is less than 1 so we append the name of the next web page and proceed back through the routine again.

```
txtPreview.Text = outresult
TabControl1.SelectTab(1)
btnPreview.Text = "Preview"
End Sub
```

What are we doing to finish up the processing of the Preview function? We have the processed web page text in the "outresult" variable, so we assign that to txtPreview.Text so that we can preview the output. We have a problem, though. You know from the first paragraph in this chapter that "the 'Preview Results' tab contains a large multi-line scrolling textbox," but you have not been told the name of it - that would be "txtPreview." In order to display that tab, we perform a SelectTab and use index 1 (second tab). We also set the Text for btnPreview back to "Preview" (remember, we had set it to "Please wait …").

SIDE TRIP Let's recap what we have done. As previously mentioned, you can view the source of any web site, and it will look similar to the code shown below. Yes, this is a portion of the LinkEmUp EBooks page.

```
<span class="showHere">You are here: </span><a href="/" class="pathway">Home</a> <img
src="/templates/beez5/images/system/arrow.png" alt="" /> <span>LinkEmUp Published
EBooks</span></div>
</div>
<div class="left1 leftbigger" id="nav"><div class="moduletable_menu">
<h3><span class="backh"><span class="backh2"><span class="backh3">This
Site</span></span></span></h3><ul class="menu">
<li class="item-435"><a href="/" >Home</a></li><li class="item-233"><a href="/login"
>Login</a></li><li class="item-448"><a href="/administrator" target="_blank" >Site
Administrator</a></li><li class="item-469"><a href="/projects" >Projects</a></li><li class="item-
483"><a href="http://astore.amazon.com/puliemup-20" >My Amazon Store</a></li><li class="item-
472"><a href="/bail-management" >Bail Bond</a></li><li class="item-480"><a href="/mobile-app-
development" >Mobile App Development</a> … <a href="/press-release-menu" >Press Release
Listing</a></li><li class="item-482 current active"><a href="/linkemup-published-ebooks" >LinkEmUp
Published EBooks</a></li><li class="item-484"><a href="http://blog.linkemup.us" >LinkEmUp
Blog</a></li></ul>
</div></div><!-- end navi -->
<div id="wrapper2" ><div id="main">
<div id="system-message-container">
</div><div class="item-page">
<h2><a href="/linkemup-published-ebooks">      EBooks (Publishing div)</a></h2>
```

```
<ul class="actions"><li class="print-icon">
<a href="/linkemup-published-ebooks?tmpl=component&amp;print=1&amp;page=" title="Print"
onclick="window.open(this.href,'win2','status=no,toolbar=no,scrollbars=yes,titlebar=no,menubar=no,resiza
ble=yes,width=640,height=480,directories=no,location=no'); return false;" rel="nofollow"><img
src="/media/system/images/printButton.png" alt="Print" /></a></li>
<li class="email-icon"><a
href="/component/mailto/?tmpl=component&amp;template=beez5&amp;link=7cff5138f0c6c6908df825c6
e73d73e0e003ba96" title="Email"
onclick="window.open(this.href,'win2','width=400,height=350,menubar=yes,resizable=yes'); return
false;"><img src="/media/system/images/emailButton.png" alt="Email" /></a></li></ul>
<dl class="article-info"><dt class="article-info-term">Details</dt>
<dd class="category-name">Category: <a href="/linkemup-published-ebooks/78-
projects">Projects</a> </dd>
<dd class="published">  Published on Wednesday, 29 January 2014 20:38  </dd>
<dd class="createdby">   Written by Administrator</dd>
<dd class="hits">Hits: 547</dd></dl><p> LinkEmUp Publishes EBooks</p>
<p>We have created Bible study material aimed at high school age and young adults. This material will be
spread across ten volumes and will cover five or six lessons per EBook. The EBooks are available in Kindle,
Nook, and other formats. See below for the list and links where these can be purchased.</p>
… Next &gt;</a></li>
</ul></div></div><!-- end main --></div><!-- end wrapper -->
<div class="wrap"></div></div> <!-- end contentarea --></div><!-- back -->
</div><!-- all --><div id="footer-outer"><div id="footer-sub">
<div id="footer">
<p>Powered by <a href="http://www.joomla.org/">Joomla!&#174;</a></p>
</div><!-- end footer -->
```

After we run the program on it

Scraping Information	Preview Results

			View
Web pages URL	www.linkemup.us		Preview
Additional DIVs		Web pages to process	Processed Text
		index.php? option=com_content&view=article	
Additional tags	&gt;		Write
Web characters . TO	Kindle, Nook, Others (Smashwords), Google Play,		Close
File storage location			
Target text begins after	LinkEmUp Blog		
Target text ends before	Powered by Joomla		

we see …

--http://www.linkemup.us/index.php?option=com_content&view=article&id=103--

EBooks (Publishing div)
Details
Category: Projects
Published on Wednesday, 29 January 2014 20:38
Written by Administrator
Hits: 556
LinkEmUp Publishes EBooks
We have created Bible study material aimed at high school age and young adults. This material will be spread across ten volumes and will cover five or six lessons per EBook. The EBooks are available in , , and other formats. See below for the list and links where these can be purchased.

Control Your Windows 7 View: Use a Single Wallpaper Across All of Your Screens

Complete, Responsive, Mobile App Design Using Visual Studio: Integrating MySQL Database into your web page (Free 2/21,22,23 through KDP Select)

HTML5, CSS3, Javascript and JQuery Mobile Programming: Beginning to End Cross-Platform App Design

Making the Most of Your Money in a Recovering EconomyFree at Smashwords and

Vol 1 - You Are the Potter's Clay: Mold Your Spirit with a study in Proverbs

Vol 2 - You Are the Potter's Clay: Mold Your Spirit with a study in Matthew

Vol 3 - You Are the Potter's Clay: Mold Your Spirit with a study in John

Vol 4 - You Are the Potter's Clay: Mold Your Spirit with another study in John

Vol 5 - You Are the Potter's Clay: Mold Your Spirit with a study in Hebrews

Shop Amazon - Top Rated in Store++ Shop Amazon - Movers & Shakers in Store ++ Shop Amazon - Hot New Releases in Store ++ Shop Amazon - Best Sellers in Store ++ Sign up for Amazon prime benefits

Next

Notice the use of the additional tag and the web characters. Since the HTML for the links was removed, it left the link text for the different book sites. We remove the link text with the four lines of "web characters." There was also a ">" left at the end of the "Next" word, so we removed that using the "Additional tags" option. More "web character" entries could have been used to remove the "monetization" Amazon text, the word "Next," and a couple more changes, but I am sure that you get the idea of how useful this can be.

That was a lot of work, and we have only been through the Preview button. Don't worry, though, the Write button uses the same logic plus a little extra code to write the results to a file.

Write Button

When looking at the code behind btnWrite, we will be leaving out much of the detail due to the exact code structure and logic when compared to the Preview function. You will be presented with all of the code, should you desire to type it in. It is suggested that, if you are using the code entry opportunity to better understand it, you should copy the code previously typed into the Preview button and modify as necessary. Let's begin with the MouseDown event ...

```
Private    Sub    btnWrite_MouseDown(sender    As    System.Object,    e    As
System.Windows.Forms.MouseEventArgs)
    btnWrite.Text = "Please wait ..."
    End Sub
```

Now we get into the code behind the Click event ...

```
Private Sub btnWrite_Click(sender As System.Object, e As System.EventArgs)
    ' This will write complete text files and display processed text in second tab
    Dim baseurl As String = txtURL.Text
```

```vbnet
If (txtFile.Text.Trim() <> "") Then
baseurl = baseurl.Replace("\\", "/")
If (Not baseurl.EndsWith("/")) Then
baseurl = baseurl + "/"
End If
If (Not baseurl.ToLower().StartsWith("http")) Then
baseurl = "http://" + baseurl
End If
' change list of URLs into array
Dim pgs As List(Of String) = New List(Of String)
pgs.AddRange(txtPages.Lines)
Dim strResult As String = ""
Dim progresult As String = ""
Dim outresult As String = "--" + baseurl + pgs(0).ToString() + "--" + vbCrLf + vbCrLf
Dim outfile As String = "--" + baseurl + pgs(0).ToString() + "--" + vbCrLf + vbCrLf
Dim charloc As Integer = 0
Dim endloc As Integer = 0
Dim y As Integer = 0
Dim delstr As String = ""
For x As Integer = 0 To pgs.Count() - 1
Dim objResponse As WebResponse
Dim objRequest As WebRequest = System.Net.HttpWebRequest.Create(baseurl +
pgs(x).ToString())
objResponse = objRequest.GetResponse()
Using sr As StreamReader = New StreamReader(objResponse.GetResponseStream())
strResult = sr.ReadToEnd()
' Close and clean up the StreamReader
sr.Close()
End Using
If cboView.SelectedItem = "Processed Text" Then
' Remove scripts
strResult = Regex.Replace(strResult, "<script.*?</script>", "",
RegexOptions.Singleline And RegexOptions.IgnoreCase)
' Remove inline stylesheets
strResult = Regex.Replace(strResult, "<style.*?</style>", "", RegexOptions.Singleline
And RegexOptions.IgnoreCase)
' remove DIVs here, if any
If txtDivs.Text.Trim() <> "" Then
Dim dvs As List(Of String) = New List(Of String)
dvs.AddRange(txtDivs.Lines)
For y = 0 To dvs.Count() - 1
strResult = Regex.Replace(strResult, "<div id='" & dvs(y).ToString() & ".*?</div>",
"", RegexOptions.Singleline And RegexOptions.IgnoreCase)
Next y
End If
' remove other tags, if any
If txtTags.Text.Trim() <> "" Then
Dim tgs As List(Of String) = New List(Of String)
tgs.AddRange(txtTags.Lines)
For y = 0 To tgs.Count() - 1
strResult = Regex.Replace(strResult, tgs(y).ToString() + ".*?</div>", "",
RegexOptions.Singleline And RegexOptions.IgnoreCase)
Next
End If
```

```
' Remove HTML tags
strResult = Regex.Replace(strResult, "</?[a-z][0-9]*[^<>]*>", "")
' Remove HTML comments
strResult = Regex.Replace(strResult, "<!--(.|\\s)*?-->", "")
' Remove Doctype
strResult = Regex.Replace(strResult, "<!(.|\\s)*?>", "")
' if web character replacement, it goes here
If txtChars.Text.Trim() <> "" Then
Dim fromtext As String = ""
Dim totext As String = ""
For y = 0 To txtChars.Lines.Count() - 1
fromtext = txtChars.Lines(y).Substring(0, txtChars.Lines(y).IndexOf(","))
totext = txtChars.Lines(y).Substring(txtChars.Lines(y).IndexOf(",") + 1)
strResult = strResult.Replace(fromtext, totext)
Next y
End If
End If
If txtBegin.Text.Trim() <> "" Then
charloc = strResult.IndexOf(txtBegin.Text.Trim())
' read each line at top and delete as long as it is blank
progresult = strResult.Substring(charloc + 17)
If txtEnd.Text.Trim() <> "" Then
endloc = progresult.IndexOf(txtEnd.Text.Trim())
progresult = progresult.Substring(1, endloc - 1)
End If
Dim delrdr As StringReader = New StringReader(progresult)
While True
delstr = delrdr.ReadLine()
If delstr Is Nothing Then
Exit While
End If
If delstr.Trim() <> "" Then
```

Until this point, nothing has changed in the processing of the web page that has been read in. This is exactly the same as the Preview code. It is at this point that we begin to see code added to enable the creation of a text file (using the variable outfile) containing the same output that we see in the Preview screen.

```
outresult = outresult + delstr + vbCrLf
outfile = outfile + delstr + vbCrLf
End If
End While
End If
Dim outdir As String = txtFile.Text.Trim()
If Not outdir.EndsWith("\\") Then
outdir = outdir + "\\"
End If
```

We are using a technique, which should be rather familiar to you by now, to check for a "\" character at the end of the directory entered ("outdir") to be used for writing the file(s). The statement was made that we will write out what we see in the Preview screen. That is almost, but not 100%, accurate. We will write what we see into individual files. If you process three pages, you will see all three in the Preview screen, but will have three files written out with the web page name.

Another difference between this code and Preview is that we are not handling the "Unmodified" selection. This is based on the belief that you do not want to write the entire web page to a file. Of course, if that were a possibility, the previous approach could be modified and would work well.

```
   Dim file As System.IO.StreamWriter = New StreamWriter(outdir + pgs(x).Replace(".",
"_") + ".txt")
   file.WriteLine(outfile)
   file.Close()
```

We have used a StreamWriter to create the file and use Replace to replace any "." characters with "_" in the file name. Using the WriteLine method of file, we write out the file. Then the file is closed, and we have finished writing the file.

```
   If x < pgs.Count() - 1 Then
   outresult = outresult + vbCrLf + vbCrLf + "--" + pgs(x + 1).ToString() + "--" + vbCrLf
+ vbCrLf
   outfile = "--" + pgs(x + 1).ToString() + "--" + vbCrLf + vbCrLf
   End If
   Next x
```

Just like the Preview approach, we are continuing with another entry in the Preview text. For the file to be written to disk, we are starting new instead of appending to the existing string. You will notice a difference between these two lines of code.

```
   txtPreview.Text = outresult
   TabControl1.SelectTab(1)
   btnPreview.Text = "Write"
   Else
   MessageBox.Show("You have to enter a write location for the file")
   End If
   End Sub
```

Other than the presence of btnWrite (versus btnPreview) and a message being displayed if Write was clicked with no location for file creation, this code is exactly the same as we saw in Preview. We have introduced a bit of new functionality with the MessageBox.Show command. As is the case with so many of the Visual Studio commands, it does exactly what it seems should be done - display the message contained in the quotes.

SIDE TRIP Since you saw the difference between the raw web site and processed text in the previous section, we will show an example of the additional functionality added to btnWrite. To produce the files shown below, we entered three web pages into the program and used "C:\Outweb" in the txtFile textbox. If desired, the code could be added to check for the existence of the directory entered and create it if necessary. In this instance, we are expecting the directory to exist.

Name	Date modified	Type	Size
associnscience_aspx.txt	6/14/2014 12:29 PM	Text Document	4 KB
businessadministration_aspx.txt	6/14/2014 12:29 PM	Text Document	3 KB
cosmetology_aspx.txt	6/14/2014 12:29 PM	Text Document	2 KB

5 THE JAVA DESKTOP PROJECT

Java may be the sole reason that you purchased this book. Then again, you may be a C# or VB programmer who will be using this as an introduction to the Java language. In either case, I have excellent news for you - the end result of this chapter will be a complete application coupled with an excellent learning opportunity.

For this project, we will be using the NetBeans **I**ntegrated **D**evelopment **E**nvironment (IDE) version 7.4. When you look at the link provided, there are various options and versions to choose from. The minimum that you will need is "Java SE," although you could download the "all" package to allow programming in HTML5, C/C++, PHP and other languages (and features). The version number is also not important - the most current version as of this writing is 8.0. Is there a cost? Only if you choose to donate since NetBeans is developed under the open source licensing model.

Once you have NetBeans installed, you will create a new JavaFX project by clicking on File - New Project. A screen similar to below will be shown (yes, the screen shows options above and beyond the "JavaSE" download).

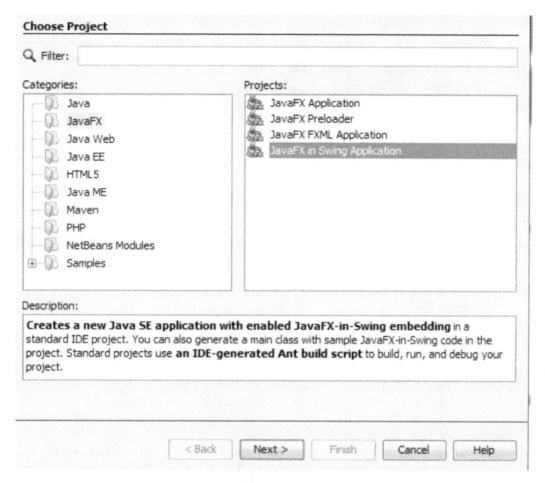

Select JavaFX and then "Swing Application" in the right pane. What is "swing" and why did we select it? Excellent question. "Swing" provides access to user interface features that we are designing. Click "Next."

The next screen will allow naming of the project (WebScraper) and selection of the location. I have a VersioningJava directory on my hard drive, whereas you may choose to use a flash drive. I would mention floppy disk, but I hope those are way in your past, and you may not even know what they are. Notice that the JavaFX platform is already selected along with the option to create the main class. These defaults should be fine. Click "Finish" and you are ready to begin on this Java journey.

We are now back in the NetBeans IDE and you should see Proj/Files/Services tabs in the upper left window pane. Select "Proj" if it is not already selected and the newly created project will be displayed. Note that I named mine WebScraper2 because the WebScraper project used for this demonstration already exists. Yours should be named "WebScraper." As shown below, you can expand out the main project, source packages and Libraries to view the default items included in the project. You can also review the default java source by clicking on the .java file and Source window which will be displayed to the right.

Now we get to start adding forms and functionality. Right-click on WebScraper under "Source Packages"

and then place your mouse over "New ..." to display the menu shown below.

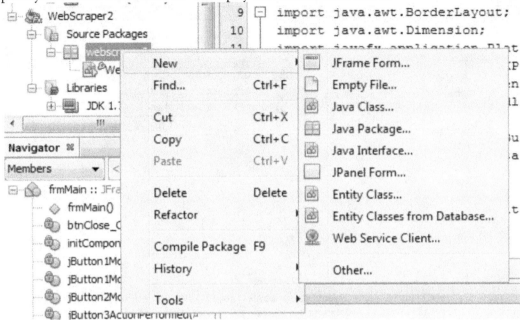

Left-clicking on "JFrame Form" will bring up a dialog box where you will have the opportunity to name the new form. Type in "frmMain" and click Finish. Now you will see an empty form in the right pane (design mode). You may be thinking "hmmm ... we sure have a long way to go before this looks like the other screens." You would be correct; but we have to start at the beginning. Prepare yourself for a whirlwind of design and coding activity ...

First, you will need the base container for this entire application - a TabbedPane. To the right of your design window you should see a window labeled "Palette." This contains all of your containers and controls which will be used in this Java program. Did you notice the initial size of this control? It would seem to be quite small for our purposes, so we will resize it and set some other items. With the JTabbedPane1 selected, on the lower right side you will see a "Properties" window. The first item to change is the name (tabMain). Next, change the preferredSize to 815,485. Be sure the Horizontal Size is set to Default, Vertical Size is set to 485 and Horizontal Resizable is checked. Finally, you may notice that the TabbedPane is not flush with the top left corner of the JFrame; double-click on the "margins" and set them to 0. It looks quite plain so far - it is time to add some nice looking containers and controls.

Now we get to add the tabs which will enable the dual functionality of our WebScraper program. Drag two Panel objects from the Swing Containers Palette to the top of the TabbedPane. This will create the two tabs for you. Now we need to properly name and label these tabs. Select tab 1 and change the Tab Title (under Properties-Layout) to "Scraping Information" and leave the rest of the properties at the default setting. On tab 2 set the Title to "Preview Results."

So far, you have done quite a bit of setup, but it does not look like much work has been put into it. The two tabs, with labels look like the screen shot below.

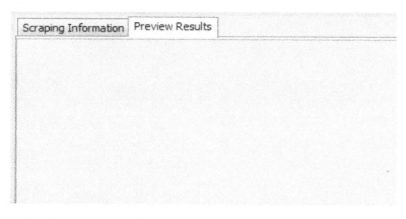

Next, we add nine labels, four text fields, four scroll panes, a combo box and three buttons to the "Scraping Information" tab so that it looks like

Well, that was quick and easy. Although it was not as quick as a snap of the fingers, it was rather easy to drag the 21 controls from the "Swing Controls" section of the Palette. Positioning them is not as easy, although item layout is much easier when you right-click on an empty space and select "Layout-Free Design."

Now that we have all of the controls on screen. We will set the specific properties for each. Follow along with the table below to set them up.

Label	Component name	Properties
Web Pages URL	jTextField1	Name = txtURL
		Horizontal Resizable = checked
Additional DIVs	jTextArea1	Rows = 5
		Name = txtDivs
Additional tags	jTextArea2	Rows = 5
		Name = txtTags

47

Web characters, TO	jTextArea3	Rows = 5
		Name = txtChars
Web pages to process	jTextArea4	Columns = 20
		Rows = 5
		Name = lstPages
File storage location	jTextField2	Name = txtFile
		Horizontal Resizable = checked
Target text begins after	jTextField3	Name = txtBegins
		Horizontal Resizable = checked
Target text ends before	jTextField4	txtEnds
		Horizontal Resizable = checked
Preview	jButton1	Background = 255,255,0
		Text = Preview
		Contentareafilled = unchecked
		Name = btnPreview
		Opaque = checked
		Vertical size = 32
		Horizontal Resizable = checked
Write	jButton2	Background = 51,255,0
		Text = Write
		Contentareafilled = unchecked
		Name = btnWrite
		Opaque = checked
		Vertical size = 32
		Horizontal Resizable = checked
Close	jButton3	Background = 255,27,0
		Text = Close
		Contentareafilled = unchecked
		Name = btnClose
		Opaque = checked
		Vertical size = Default
		Horizontal Resizable = checked
View	jComboBox1	Model = Unmodified, Processed text
		Name = cboView
		Horizontal Size = 107

Since you have entered the properties as shown above, the "Scraping Information" tab should look like the previous screen shot. It looks good but it is about as functional as your pet rock (if you don't remember floppy disks, I am sure that you won't remember these either). We get to change that now, though. Let's take a look at the code behind our components.

Do we have any functionality behind the text elements on the screen? No, we do not. They are simply containers for the data that we will be typing into our program. We will use the contents of these containers in the processing of our web pages.

If you have been through chapters two and four, you have seen the "Events" tab which allows attaching code to specific actions tied to a screen element. In this case, you can create a new area for typing your code by clicking the ellipsis beside of the event name (...) and then "Add." This will allow you to name the routine. The general procedure is to use the name of the component followed with the name of the event (i.e.

"jButton1MouseClicked"). Let's start with btnPreview and its functionality - mouseClicked and mousePressed.

```
private void jButton1MousePressed(java.awt.event.MouseEvent evt) {
jButton1.setText("Please wait ...");
}
```

This, quite simply, changes the text displayed on the button to "Please Wait ..." In most cases on today's faster computers, the effect is a quick blink and not really noticeable. For larger web pages and slower computers, this change is necessary to let the user know that the button has been clicked and the page is processing.

```
private void jButton1MouseClicked(java.awt.event.MouseEvent evt) {
// This will display complete text or processed text in the second tab
String baseurl = jTextField1.getText();
```

Notice that our first line of code is a comment stating what will be done with the output of our method. In the next line we are declaring the baseurl variable as string and assigning to it the value of the string typed into the "txtURL" textbox of our screen. The getText() function is what we use to assign the value.

```
baseurl.replace("\\", "/");
if(!baseurl.endsWith("/"))
{
baseurl += "/";
}
if(!baseurl.toLowerCase().startsWith("http"))
{
baseurl = "http://" + baseurl;
}
```

In these lines of code, we have used the "replace" method to replace the "\" character with the other slash - "/". Did you notice that the first parameter in that statement has two backslash ("\") characters? That character is special and it is used for the purpose of "escaping" other characters. In other words, it can change the meaning of any character it is used in front of.

Why did we double the "\" character, though? By using two of these together, the Java runtime knows that we actually mean to use the "\" character itself. Java runtime? Hmmmm, this is the first that I have heard of that. We won't get too technical with the definition, but the code that you see here, and type in yourself, is not executed by the IDE program that you are running. Java code is packaged into a JAR file for distribution to the recipient audience and the Java runtime loads and executes that file.

Now that we have that basic definition out of the way, let's dive into the rest of that section of code. You will notice the use of the endsWith, startsWith, and toLowerCase methods. These perform exactly what it seems like they should. With the endsWith, we are checking for an ending "/" character on the string. If it does not exist (this is indicated by the "!" at the beginning of the string), we will add it with a simple "append" command. The logical next step is to convert the entire string to lower case using toLowerCase. This will ensure that we do not need to check for the existence of "http" or hTTp" or "HTTP."

I am sure that you get the picture. The string can be typed any way that the user desires, so we make accommodations for that capability. Once again, we are checking that it does NOT start with "http" and then add http:// to the front of the string using another simple append.

```
// change list of URLs into an array
String pgs[] = jTextArea4.getText().split("\\n");
```

Notice that we have placed another comment to indicate the purpose of this line of code. We use a variable type of String. As you have experienced so far, this means basically what it says - the variable "pgs" is a list of strings. In the next line of code we populate that list with each line that was entered into the jTextArea4 textbox (remember, this has multi-line turned on). What have we done now? If we typed ten individual web pages into the box, we now have the "pgs" string array populated with ten items. We accomplished that population with a single split command which separates the lines based on the newline (\n) character.

So far you haven't been introduced to an array. Notice our initialization and use of the variable called "pgs" which is defined with brackets after the name. This defines that variable as an array of strings. What is an array? Basically, it is a list. Because of this, we are able to get the text and populate the array with each individual line.

```
String strResult = "";
String progresult = "";
String outresult = "--" + baseurl + pgs[0] + "--\r\n\r\n";
int charloc = 0;
int endloc = 0;
int y = 0;
String delstr = "";
```

You have already learned that variables need to be defined before they can be used. That is what we are doing with these seven lines of code. In this section of code, you also get to experience the use of that array. Notice that we are appending "--, " baseurl, pages[0] and another string with some "escaped" characters. First, why do we use [0] behind the "pgs" variable? Because it is an array and we are selecting the first item in that array. But this is zero, shouldn't the first be a "1"? Not in the Java language, it is a zero-based language. This means that arrays start with item 0 and locations within a string start with 0. Yes, it requires a new mindset, but you can get the hang of it.

To end the current line, we use "\r\n" escape strings. Since we are using two of these, we end the current line and add a blank line beneath it.

```
for(int x=0;x<pgs.length;x++)
{
```

Now we are in "the meat" of the program, so it is time to slow the pace down a bit and give more detail in the functionality explanations. If you have gone through previous chapters and built the functioning applications, you will probably recognize some of the code shown here - it is the same base logic with added functionality and capabilities afforded by a user interface.

The line above is known as a "FOR loop." The purpose is to begin with the first line in the "web pages to process" textbox and perform some processing with it. Once the end of the loop is reached, it will check to see if more lines exist and perform the process again and again until there are no more lines. Below that line of code you see an open brace ({). This indicates to the program that the loop processing starts now and goes until the matching close brace (}) is reached. Because of Ebook formatting rules, all text has to be left aligned, so it is not so easy to see where the end bracket happens to be. In your Netbeans editor (or whatever else you may be using), the sections should be indented and easily identifiable.

```
try
{
URL objRequest = new URL(baseurl + pgs[x].toString());
URLConnection midrdr = objRequest.openConnection();
BufferedReader in = new BufferedReader(new InputStreamReader(midrdr.getInputStream()));
```

You may be thinking "Hey, there's a TRY statement. I have seen that before." You would be correct with this pondering. We use a try/catch block to catch any errors, and then move into the main functionality of the program.

The next three lines work together to load the current web page, as it was entered into the "web pages to process" textbox. First, we create a URL object (named objRequest) which is used to store the response received from the web page as it is loaded. The second variable, midrdr, is a URLConnection which is populated with an openConnection to retrieve the web page from its host. We determine the **U**niform **R**esource **L**ocator by combining the entry into the "web pages URL" (baseurl) with the current line that we are processing, indicated by "x." Finally, we get to use the getInputStream() method of midrdr to read the page contents into the BufferedReader named "in." Now that we have the web page in memory, it is time to do something with it.

```
while((progresult = in.readLine()) != null)
{
strResult += progresult + "\r";
}
```

This is another statement that may be familiar to you from chapters one or three. The purpose of this "while" statement is to read through each line of the web page that we have just loaded and store it into a variable named progresult. With each iteration through this loop, we build the strResult variable and add a new line character (\r) at the end of each line.

```
in.close();
}
catch (Exception e)
{
}
```

Now we close the reader named "in" and terminate the try ... catch statement. We could analyze the exception (e) if an error is encountered and perform specific functions based on the type.

```
if(jComboBox1.getSelectedIndex() == 1)
{
```

We have just opened an "if" statement. This has the same function as your logical decision making that is performed every day - if I have a couple of donuts for breakfast, (then) I need to walk an extra mile during lunch. You could also add to that - "(else) I can walk my dog an extra mile tonight." That covers the simplicity of an if-then-else statement although you can string these together and create some monster-sized logic. If you see a need for more than a few of these strung together, the "switch ... case" statement will probably be a much better option.

Anyway, back to our "if" statement. This is looking at the selection made with the "dropdown" which is labeled "jComboBox1." Since you have only two options in this box, we check to see if "Processed text" was selected. If it was, then we process a section of code. If the other option - "Unmodified" was selected, a separate section of code is executed. Once again, the code between the brackets is executed.

```
//Remove Scripts
strResult = strResult.replaceAll("<script.*?</script>", "");
// Remove inline style sheets
strResult = strResult.replaceAll("<style.*?</style>", "");
```

If you are an advanced student or seasoned programmer in any language, the functionality of the code shown above may be rather obvious. In case it is not, we will go into some detail. First, let's note a difference between the replaceAll function and other, more familiar, append-style functions. Notice that each statement builds on the previous statement to parse out more of our raw page by replacing certain strings with nothing ("").

Now that we have a small explanation out of the way, we will look at the "Remove Scripts" statement. We examine the strResult variable for all occurrences of "<script...</script>" and remove them. Now, you may be wondering what the ".*?" is used for. The usage of ".*?" indicates that anything, or nothing, can occur between the beginning and ending script tags. The end result is the removal of all script, whether it is JavaScript, VBScript or anything else contained within HTML <script></script> tags.

The code for removing inline stylesheets follows the same principle that you have already seen - replaceAll. The only difference is the removal of anything within the HTML <style></style> tags.

SIDE TRIP What is a real life example of the cleanup that we have done so far? I am glad that you were pondering that thought. You can load any functional site on the web and view source. In that listing you will see lines such as

<script src="http://passets-cd.pinterest.com/webapp/js/app/desktop/bundle.c2facd24.js"></script>

And

<style>a:lang(ar),a:lang(kk-arab),a:lang(mzn),a:lang(ps),a:lang(ur){text-decoration:none}
/* cache key: enwiki:resourceloader:filter:minify-css:7:3904d24a08aa08f6a68dc338f9be277e */</style>

These are the lines removed due to the HTML tags that are contained in them. You may recognize these explanations if you have already completed previous chapters. Yes, the lines and explanations are quite similar.

```
//remove DIVs here, if any
String dvs[] = jTextArea1.getText().split("\\n");
```

In our Java program, we deviate from the "IF" statements used in the previous chapters. Instead, we are using an array of strings, as indicated by the brackets([ ]) following the String declaration. We convert the jTextArea into an array using the "split" function of the getText() command. By splitting on the newline character (\n), we are placing each line into its own iteration of the array. You will recall from previous chapters that we double the "\" character so that the Java runtime properly considers the intended newline character. As a matter of fact, if you compare this section of code to the other versions, it takes one line to do what they accomplish in four.

```
for(y=0;y<dvs.length;y++)
{
if(!dvs[y].toString().isEmpty())
{
strResult = strResult.replaceAll("<div id=" + dvs[y].toString() + ".*?</div>", "");
}
}
```

You should be familiar with the "for" loop and the replaceAll method. Notice that we are replacing a specific DIV which was entered into the "jTextArea1" textbox. This gives us the opportunity to remove as many DIVs as necessary. As long as we use a begin and end text string, the only DIVs that will need to be removed will be between those two strings. Also notice the two closing braces in this code. It is closing the "for" loop and the "if" statement. The next line of code is where the processing continues in case the "if" statement is actually false (empty txtDivs textbox).

```
//remove other tags
String tgs[] = jTextArea2.getText().split("\\n");
for(y=0;y<tgs.length;y++)
{
if(!tgs[y].toString().isEmpty())
```

```
{
strResult = strResult.replaceAll(tgs[y].toString() + ".*?</div>", "");
}
}
```

This uses the exact same logic as the DIVs, except that it is used for specific HTML tags. The pages that you are extracting the text from may contain non-breaking spaces. In that case, you would enter " " into the txtTags textbox. Others that you may want to use are "<" (<), "&" (&) and more. Whether this functionality is needed will depend on which, if any, of these are used within the desired web page.

```
//remove HTML tags
strResult = strResult.replaceAll("</?[a-z][a-z0-9]*[^<>]*>", "");
//remove HTML comments
strResult = strResult.replaceAll("<!--(.|\\s)*?-->", "");
//remove doctype
strResult = strResult.replaceAll("<!(.|\\s)*?>", "");
```

Now we get to remove the standard HTML tags (between the brackets) using some of the deeper functionality that replaceAll can accomplish - pattern matching. The character "<" has to occur to begin the tag, while the "/" can occur 0 or 1 time. The "?" wildcard is the indicator of 0 or 1 occurrence of the character. Characters a to z and 0 to 9 can occur any number of times - this is the meaning of the "*" wildcard character. The next three characters inside of the brackets are explicit characters that can occur in the string, "^< >" but the "^" in front indicates that the bracket characters will not be replaced inside of the HTML tag. The closing character is the last in the HTML tag - ">"

What will this replace? It replaces all beginning HTML tags along with the matching end tags. Okay then, why is additional processing required? It leaves the text between those tags. This also does not touch the non-standard tags such as comments and doctype. The next line, as the comment states, will remove any HTML comments. In-line HTML comments begin with "<!--" so that is the beginning string searched for, and end with "-->" The included string "(.|\\s)" followed by the wildcard "*" means that any characters (other than a newline) and spaces can exist between the beginning and end string. The Doctype tag begins with "<!" and it follows a similar process by replacing any doctype tags with an empty string.

```
//if web character replacement it goes here
String cts[] = jTextArea3.getText().split("\\n");
String fromtext = "";
String totext = "";
for(y=0;y<cts.length;y++)
{
if(!cts[y].toString().isEmpty())
{
fromtext = cts[y].toString().substring(0, cts[y].toString().indexOf(","));
totext = cts[y].toString().substring(cts[y].toString().indexOf(",")+1);
strResult = strResult.replace(fromtext, totext);
}
}
```

Using the "webscraper" program, you have the ability to replace any strings with anything else that you may desire. Maybe the scraped pages have a number of employees set to 100 and you want to automatically change that to 110. If so, you would enter 100,110 in a single line of the jTextArea3 textbox.

That is the purpose, but how is it accomplished? Good pondering. First, we have to break the "from" and "to" text out of the comma-delimited line. In both cases, we look for the comma with "indexOf" and use substring to parse out the two variables. Now that we have the from/to text, it is a simple Replace on the strResult variable. Notice that we are closing the "for," "if" and the "if" that checked to see if "Processed Text" had been selected. If not, processing falls through to the following "else" procedure.

```java
if(!jTextField3.getText().isEmpty())
{
charloc = strResult.indexOf(jTextField3.getText().trim());
progresult = strResult.substring(charloc + 17);
```

So far in this routine, we have determined that something was entered into the txtBegin textbox. We search for that string within strResult using indexOf and store that into the "charloc" variable. Now that we know the location of that beginning string, we use substring to start at the desired location within "strResult" and assign the new string to "progresult." The proper starting point is actually the found location of the "txtBegin" string plus the length of that string minus 1. Since we are only using one parameter of Substring, the result begins at that point and returns the remainder of the string.

Remember, Java is a zero-based language. This makes it necessary to subtract 1 from lengths and a few other properties.

```java
if(!jTextField4.getText().isEmpty())
{
endloc = progresult.indexOf(jTextField4.getText().trim());
progresult = progresult.substring(1, endloc-1);
}
}
```

Now we check to see if an ending string was entered. If so, we check for the existence of it within progresult using indexOf. Once again, we use substring, this time with a start and end parameter. We start at the second character (zero-based) and use the rest of the "progresult" string until it encounters the end string (minus 1).

If you were to look at the "progresult" string now, you will probably notice many undesired blank lines that were generated by all of the replace with an empty string. This is not truly desirable, so we have a routine that will read progresult one line at a time and assign the line to the "outresult" variable only if it is not empty.

```java
try
{
BufferedReader in = new BufferedReader(new StringReader(progresult));
while ((delstr = in.readLine())!= null)
{
if (!delstr.trim().isEmpty())
{
outresult += delstr + "\r\n";
}
}
}
catch (Exception e)
{
}
}
else
{
outresult += strResult;
}
```

As stated, this routine will read each line of the "progresult" variable by assigning it to a BufferedReader named "in." Within the "while" statement, we are using ReadLine to individually read each line until we have no more. The line is being read into the "delstr" string variable. Inside of the while process, we are using the isEmpty() function to determine that the line is not (!) empty. If not empty, the line is appended to the "outresult" string variable with the carriage return-line feed escape sequences. Notice the three closing braces and closing of the catch() block. This is the location to do any specific error displays, should you choose to add them. This section of code also contains the "else" side of the "Processed Text" question. If "Unmodified" is selected, there is no processing and all contents of the web page are added to the outresult string.

You may be wondering, "What purpose does 'Unprocessed' have?" Good question. As an end result, the unprocessed text is quite useless. In the beginning of the process, however, you can view this code to pick out the begin/end text, DIVs to remove, additional tags and character changes needed within the program.

```
if(x < pgs. Length - 1)
{
outresult += "\n\n--" + pgs[x+1] + "--\n\n";
strResult = "";
}
}
```

Now we have finished processing the current page. The "x" variable is the current line that we are on and it is being compared to the total pages count (minus 1). Let's say that there was only one web page entered, that would be index 0 and x is currently 0. pgs.length is 1but when we subtract 1 from that, the "if" statement is false and we fall through to the display of our results, shown below.

If two web pages were entered, and this is the first time through the routine, x is still equal to 0. The count of pgs is now 2 and zero is less than 1 so we append the name of the next web page and proceed back through the routine again.

```
jTextArea5.setText(outresult);
jTabbedPane1.setSelectedIndex(1);
jButton1.setText("Preview");
}
```

What are we doing to finish up the processing of the Preview function? We have the processed web page text in the "outresult" variable, so we assign that to txtPreview.Text in order to preview the output. We have a problem, though. You know from the first paragraph in this chapter that "the 'Preview Results' tab contains a large multi-line scrolling textbox," but you have not been told the name of it - that would be "jTextArea5." In order to display that tab, we perform a setSelectedIndex and use index 1 (second tab). We also set the Text for jButton1 back to "Preview" (remember, we had set it to "Please wait ...").

SIDE TRIP Let's recap what we have done. As previously mentioned, you can view the source of any web site, and it will look similar to the code shown below. Yes, this is a portion of the LinkEmUp EBooks page.

```
<span class="showHere">You are here: </span><a href="/" class="pathway">Home</a> <img
src="/templates/beez5/images/system/arrow.png" alt="" /> <span>LinkEmUp Published
EBooks</span></div>
</div>
<div class="left1 leftbigger" id="nav"><div class="moduletable_menu">
<h3><span class="backh"><span class="backh2"><span class="backh3">This
Site</span></span></span></h3><ul class="menu">
<li class="item-435"><a href="/" >Home</a></li><li class="item-233"><a href="/login"
>Login</a></li><li class="item-448"><a href="/administrator" target="_blank" >Site
```

Administrator</a></li><li class="item-469"><a href="/projects" >Projects</a></li><li class="item-483"><a href="http://astore.amazon.com/puliemup-20" >My Amazon Store</a></li><li class="item-472"><a href="/bail-management" >Bail Bond</a></li><li class="item-480"><a href="/mobile-app-development" >Mobile App Development</a> … <a href="/press-release-menu" >Press Release Listing</a></li><li class="item-482 current active"><a href="/linkemup-published-ebooks" >LinkEmUp Published EBooks</a></li><li class="item-484"><a href="http://blog.linkemup.us" >LinkEmUp Blog</a></li></ul>

   </div></div><!-- end navi -->

   <div id="wrapper2" ><div id="main">

   <div id="system-message-container">

   </div><div class="item-page">

   <h2><a href="/linkemup-published-ebooks">   EBooks (Publishing div)</a></h2>

   <ul class="actions"><li class="print-icon">

   <a href="/linkemup-published-ebooks?tmpl=component&print=1&page=" title="Print" onclick="window.open(this.href,'win2','status=no,toolbar=no,scrollbars=yes,titlebar=no,menubar=no,resizable=yes,width=640,height=480,directories=no,location=no'); return false;" rel="nofollow"><img src="/media/system/images/printButton.png" alt="Print" /></a></li>

   <li class="email-icon"><a href="/component/mailto/?tmpl=component&template=beez5&link=7cff5138f0c6c6908df825c6e73d73e0e003ba96" title="Email" onclick="window.open(this.href,'win2','width=400,height=350,menubar=yes,resizable=yes'); return false;"><img src="/media/system/images/emailButton.png" alt="Email" /></a></li></ul>

   <dl class="article-info"><dt class="article-info-term">Details</dt>

   <dd class="category-name">Category: <a href="/linkemup-published-ebooks/78-projects">Projects</a> </dd>

   <dd class="published"> Published on Wednesday, 29 January 2014 20:38 </dd>

   <dd class="createdby"> Written by Administrator</dd>

   <dd class="hits">Hits: 547</dd></dl><p> LinkEmUp Publishes EBooks</p>

   <p>We have created Bible study material aimed at high school age and young adults. This material will be spread across ten volumes and will cover five or six lessons per EBook. The EBooks are available in Kindle, Nook, and other formats. See below for the list and links where these can be purchased.</p>

   … Next ></a></li>

   </ul></div></div><!-- end main --></div><!-- end wrapper -->

   <div class="wrap"></div></div> <!-- end contentarea --></div><!-- back -->

   </div><!-- all --><div id="footer-outer"><div id="footer-sub">

   <div id="footer">

   <p>Powered by <a href="http://www.joomla.org/">Joomla!®</a></p>

   </div><!-- end footer -->

After we run the program on it

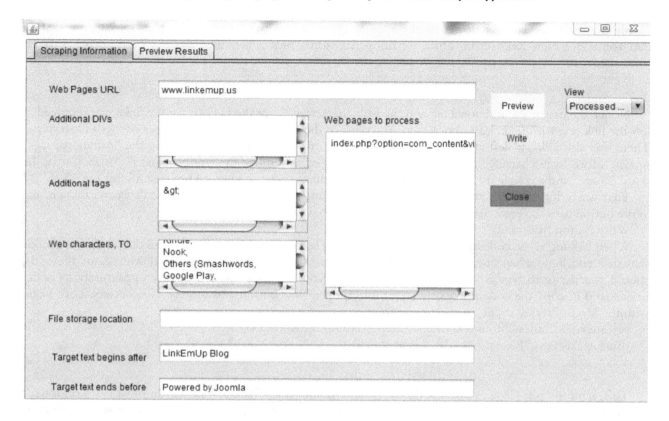

we see ...

--http://www.linkemup.us/index.php?option=com_content&view=article&id=103--

EBooks (Publishing div)
Details
Category: Projects
Published on Wednesday, 29 January 2014 20:38
Written by Administrator
Hits: 556
LinkEmUp Publishes EBooks
We have created Bible study material aimed at high school age and young adults. This material will be spread across ten volumes and will cover five or six lessons per EBook. The EBooks are available in , , and other formats. See below for the list and links where these can be purchased.
Control Your Windows 7 View: Use a Single Wallpaper Across All of Your Screens
Complete, Responsive, Mobile App Design Using Visual Studio: Integrating MySQL Database into your web page (Free 2/21,22,23 through KDP Select)
HTML5, CSS3, Javascript and JQuery Mobile Programming: Beginning to End Cross-Platform App Design
Making the Most of Your Money in a Recovering EconomyFree at Smashwords and
Vol 1 - You Are the Potter's Clay: Mold Your Spirit with a study in Proverbs
Vol 2 - You Are the Potter's Clay: Mold Your Spirit with a study in Matthew
Vol 3 - You Are the Potter's Clay: Mold Your Spirit with a study in John
Vol 4 - You Are the Potter's Clay: Mold Your Spirit with another study in John
Vol 5 - You Are the Potter's Clay: Mold Your Spirit with a study in Hebrews

Shop Amazon - Top Rated in Store++ Shop Amazon - Movers & Shakers in Store ++ Shop Amazon - Hot New Releases in Store ++ Shop Amazon - Best Sellers in Store ++ Sign up for Amazon prime benefits
Next

Notice the use of the additional tag and the web characters. Since the HTML for the links was removed, it left the link text for the different book sites. We remove the link text with the four lines of "web characters." There was also a ">" left at the end of the "Next" word, so we removed that using the "Additional tags" option. More "web character" entries could have been used to remove the "monetization" Amazon text, the word "Next," and a couple more changes, but I am sure that you get the idea of how useful this can be.

That was a lot of work, and we have only been through the Preview button. Don't worry, though, the Write button uses the same logic plus a little extra code to write the results to a file.

Write Button (jButton2)

When looking at the code behind jButton2, we will be leaving out much of the detail due to the exact code structure and logic when compared to the Preview function. You will be presented with all of the code, should you desire to type it in. It is suggested that, if you are using the code entry opportunity to better understand it, copy the code previously typed into the Preview button and modify as necessary. Let's begin with the MousePressed event …

```java
private void jButton2MousePressed(java.awt.event.MouseEvent evt) {
jButton2.setText("Please wait ...");
}
```

This, quite simply, changes the text displayed on the button to "Please Wait …" In most cases on today's faster computers, this is a quick blink and not really noticeable. For larger web pages and slower computers, this change is necessary to let the user know that the button has been clicked and the page is processing.

Now we get into the code behind the Click event …

```java
private void jButton2MouseClicked(java.awt.event.MouseEvent evt) {
if(!jTextField2.getText().isEmpty())
{
String baseurl = jTextField1.getText();
baseurl.replace("\\", "/");
if(!baseurl.endsWith("/"))
{
baseurl += "/";
}
if(!baseurl.toLowerCase().startsWith("http"))
{
baseurl = "http://" + baseurl;
}
String pgs[] = jTextArea4.getText().split("\\n");
String strResult = "";
String progresult = "";
String outresult = "--" + baseurl + pgs[0] + "--\r\n\r\n";
String outfile = "--" + pgs[0] + "--\r\n\r\n";
int charloc = 0;
int endloc = 0;
int y = 0;
String delstr = "";
for(int x=0;x<pgs.length;x++)
```

```java
{
try
{
URL objRequest = new URL(baseurl + pgs[x].toString());
URLConnection midrdr = objRequest.openConnection();
BufferedReader in = new BufferedReader(new InputStreamReader(midrdr.getInputStream()));
while((progresult = in.readLine()) != null)
{
strResult += progresult + "\r";
}
in.close();
}
catch (Exception e)
{
}
if(jComboBox1.getSelectedIndex() == 1)
{
strResult = strResult.replaceAll("<script.*?</script>", "");
strResult = strResult.replaceAll("<style.*?</style>", "");
//remove DIVs
String dvs[] = jTextArea1.getText().split("\\n");
for(y=0;y<dvs.length;y++)
{
if(!dvs[y].toString().isEmpty())
{
strResult = strResult.replaceAll("<div id=" + dvs[y].toString() + ".*?</div>", "");
}
}
//remove other tags
String tgs[] = jTextArea2.getText().split("\\n");
for(y=0;y<tgs.length;y++)
{
if(!tgs[y].toString().isEmpty())
{
strResult = strResult.replaceAll(tgs[y].toString() + ".*?</div>", "");
}
}
//remove HTML tags
strResult = strResult.replaceAll("</?[a-z][a-z0-9]*[^<>]*>", "");
//remove HTML comments
strResult = strResult.replaceAll("<!--(.|\\s)*?-->", "");
//remove doctype
strResult = strResult.replaceAll("<!(.|\\s)*?>", "");
//if web character replacement it goes here
String cts[] = jTextArea3.getText().split("\\n");
String fromtext = "";
String totext = "";
for(y=0;y<cts.length;y++)
{
```

```
if(!cts[y].toString().isEmpty())
{
fromtext = cts[y].toString().substring(0, cts[y].toString().indexOf(","));
totext = cts[y].toString().substring(cts[y].toString().indexOf(",")+1);
strResult = strResult.replace(fromtext, totext);
}
}
if(!jTextField3.getText().isEmpty())
{
charloc = strResult.indexOf(jTextField3.getText().trim());
progresult = strResult.substring(charloc + 17);
if(!jTextField4.getText().isEmpty())
{
endloc = progresult.indexOf(jTextField4.getText().trim());
progresult = progresult.substring(1, endloc-1);
}
}
try
{
BufferedReader in = new BufferedReader(new StringReader(progresult));
while ((delstr = in.readLine())!= null)
{
if (!delstr.trim().isEmpty())
{
```

Until this point, nothing has changed in the processing of the web page that has been read in. This is exactly the same as the Preview code. It is at this point that we begin to see code added to enable the creation of a text file (using the variable outfile) containing the same output that we see in the Preview screen.

```
outresult += delstr + "\r\n";
outfile += delstr + "\r\n";
strResult = "";
}
}
}
catch (Exception e)
{
}
}
else
{
outresult += strResult;
}
String outdir = jTextField2.getText().trim();
if(!outdir.endsWith("\\"))
{
outdir += "\\";
}
```

We are using a technique, which should be rather familiar to you by now, to check for a "\" character at the end of the directory entered ("outdir") to be used for writing the file(s). The statement was made that we will write out what we see in the Preview screen. That is almost, but not 100%, accurate. We will write what we see into individual files. If you process three pages, you will see all three in the Preview screen, but will have three files written out with the web page name.

Another difference between this code and Preview is that we are not handling the "Unmodified" selection. This is based on the belief that you do not want to write the entire web page to a file. Of course, if that were a possibility, the previous approach would work well.

```
try
{
PrintWriter file = new PrintWriter(outdir + pgs[x].replace(".", "_") + ".txt");
file.write(outfile);
file.close();
}
catch (Exception e)
{
}
```

We have used a PrintWriter to create the file and use replace to replace any "." characters with "_" in the file name. Using the write method of file, we write out the file. Then the file is closed, and we have finished writing the file.

```
if(x < pgs. Length - 1)
{
outresult += "\n\n--" + pgs[x+1] + "--\n\n";
outfile = "\n\n--" + pgs[x+1] + "--\n\n";
}
}
```

Just like the Preview approach, we are continuing with another entry in the Preview text. For the file to be written to disk, we are starting new instead of appending to the existing string. You will notice a difference between these two lines of code.

```
jTextArea5.setText(outresult);
jTabbedPane1.setSelectedIndex(1);
jButton2.setText("Write");
}
else
{
JOptionPane.showMessageDialog(rootPane, "You have to enter a write location for the file");
}
}
```

Other than the presence of btnWrite (versus btnPreview) and a message being displayed if Write was clicked with no location for file creation, this code is exactly the same as we saw in Preview. We have introduced a bit of new functionality with the showMessageDialog command. As is the case with so many of the Java commands, it does exactly what it seems should be done - display the message contained in the quotes.

SIDE TRIP Since you saw the difference between the raw web site and processed text in the previous section, we will show an example of the additional functionality added to jButton2. To produce the files shown below, we entered three web pages into the program and used "C:\Outweb" in the jTextField2 textbox. If desired, the code could be added to check for the existence of the directory entered and create it if necessary. In this instance, we are expecting the directory to exist.

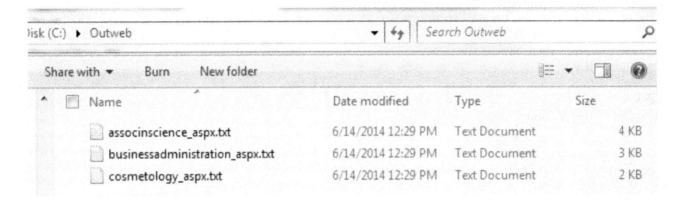

6 EXCEL VBA CODE FOR CONSOLE PROGRAM AUTOMATION

This is the fourth language used in this book - Visual Basic for Applications. We will use Excel and macro programming to automate the processing of either of the console programs. First, a bit of introductory information - we will be using Microsoft Excel 2010 and a spreadsheet that appears as the screen shot below.

	A
1	Page name
2	index
3	cars
4	houses
5	land
6	Apartments
7	
8	

To add the macro code, you would go to the Visual Basic editor (ALT+F11) and then click on Modules and Insert Module. Put the code shown below and you are ready to go.

```
Sub pagescrape()
currval = ActiveCell.Value
ChDir ("c:\rcvurls")
While currval <> ""
Shell ("webscrapper " & currval)
Application.Wait (Now + TimeValue("0:00:03"))
ActiveCell.Offset(1, 0).Activate
currval = ActiveCell.Value
Wend
End Sub
```

In the example Excel sheet, you would place the cursor in cell A2 and run the pagescrape macro. It can be run either by clicking macros and selecting it or assigning a shortcut key and pressing the key combination to start it.

As the macro is written, you should have created a directory named "rcvurls" in your C drive. Of course, you could modify the directory name as desired.

This macro is used in combination with either of the console programs that you may have created - VB.Net or C#. It produces the same output seen at the end of the desktop program chapters. Of course, the files produced by the sample sheet shown in this chapter will produce five files named the same as the input web page names. The desktop programs, as designed in these chapters, use www.linkemup.us (which will need to be changed) and automatically append the ".aspx" extension to the file name.

Knowledge Test

The console program becomes extremely more useful by allowing the URL to be input from the command line in addition to the file extension being input by the user. These could be accomplished in either area - VB.Net/C# or Excel VBA. Can you make these modifications? (hint: you will need to modify both programs, regardless of which method is chosen)

You may also notice, as progress is made through the desktop programs, that additional processing was intentionally included for experience and clarification. Taking a logical approach would allow removal of some of the code in these programs. Can you find the sections of code that may not be absolutely necessary?

A - ADDITIONAL RESOURCES THAT YOU MAY ENJOY

Learning C# for beginners
http://www.ehow.com/how_6942912_learn-c_-beginners.html

CSharp Study (Blogspot)
http://csharpstudysimple.blogspot.com/

Visual C# Resources (MSDN)
http://msdn.microsoft.com/en-us/vstudio/hh341490.aspx

How to study Visual Basic
http://www.ehow.com/how_5108786_study-visual-basic.html

Online VB training from freetutes
http://visualbasic.freetutes.com/

How to start programming VB.Net
http://howtostartprogramming.com/vb-net/

Various articles on Java programming
http://sourcecodemania.com/category/java-programming/

Learning Java (Netbeans)
https://netbeans.org/kb/articles/learn-java.html

Java tutorials (Oracle)
http://docs.oracle.com/javase/tutorial/

Microsoft development tools
http://dev.windows.com/en-us/

Netbeans download
https://netbeans.org/downloads/6.7.1/

B - SOURCE CODE LINKS

The link to download the source for the programs you have seen is
https://wwwords.biz/WebScraperBook/WebScraper.zip
https://wwwords.biz/WebScraperBook/WebScraperJava.zip
These files come in zipped format. The first contains for .Net projects and cover the first four chapters - C# command line, C# Desktop, VB.Net command line and VB.Net desktop. In order to run an individual project from within Visual Studio, you should right-click the project (WebScraper, for example) and left-click on "Set as Startup Project." Now this will be the project executed when you click F5 (Start Debugging).

The second contains the Java program designed in NetBeans. If you have Netbeans installed, unzip the file into its own folder and open the project using File-Open Project and open the WebScraper project in that directory.

If you choose a Visual Studio version other than 2010 or a Java programming environment other than NetBeans, the logic and code contained within this book can be converted to fit, although it may be a bit of trouble to get everything in place.

As long as you are on an operating system beyond XP, you should not require a separate zip manager. If you happen to need one, 7Zip (http://7-zip.org/) is an excellent open source program to use.

ABOUT THE AUTHOR

Stephen J. Link is a "computer guy" by profession, an author by hobby, and a Layman in the study of God's Word. He has a computer support book entitled "Link Em Up On Outlook" that was published in 2004 as a paperback (renamed to "Power Outlook" in reprint). He also has over 125 articles covering various topics published on his own blog and independent sites. Various Books have been published covering a number of topics. As a programmer, he has a unique approach to help you master the ability to create the code for automating processes and adding efficiency to your client's or employer's processes.

OTHER WORKS BY STEPHEN LINK AND LINK EM UP, PUBLISHING DIVISION

Programming and Design

HTML5, CSS3, Javascript and JQuery Mobile Programming: Beginning to End Cross-Platform App Design

Complete, Responsive, Mobile App Design Using Visual Studio: Integrating MySQL Database into your web page

Four Programming Languages Creating a Complete Webscraper Application

Excel Programming through VBA: A Complete Macro Driven Excel 2010 Application

Christian Study

The Journey Along God's Road to Revelation: Complete Scripture Reading in a Year

Volume 1 of the Potter's Clay series: Mold Your Spirit with a Study in Proverbs

Volume 2 of the Potter's Clay series: Mold Your Spirit with a Study in Matthew

Volume 3 of the Potter's Clay series: Mold Your Spirit with a Study in John

Volume 4 of the Potter's Clay series: Mold Your Spirit with another Study in John

Volume 5 of the Potter's Clay series: Mold Your Spirit with a Study in Hebrews

Volume 6 of the Potter's Clay series: Mold Your Spirit with a Study in Acts

Your Computer

Control Your Windows 7 View: Use a Single Wallpaper Across All of Your Screens

Most are in Ebook format and are available across multiple platforms. You can start at https://wwwords.biz to select the book and platform needed. As time allows, these books will be made available for purchase in print.

Social connections

www.facebook.com/stephen.linkemup

www.twitter.com/slinkemup

www.linkedin.com/in/slinkemup